ROTISSERIE CHICKENS

— to the —

RESCUE!

ROTISSERIE CHICKENS

— to the —

RESCUE!

How to Use the Already-Roasted Chickens You Purchase at

the Market to Make More Than 125 Simple and Delicious Meals

CARLA FITZGERALD WILLIAMS

HYPERION NEW YORK

Library of Congress Cataloging-in-Publication Data
Williams, Carla Fitzgerald.
    Rotisserie chickens to the rescue! : how to use the already-roasted chickens you purchase at the market to make more than 125 simple and delicious meals / Carla Fitzgerald Williams.—1st ed.
       p. cm.
    ISBN: 0-7868-8804-0
    1. Cookery (Chicken) I. Title.

TX750.5.C45W58 2003
641.6'65—dc21   2003042333

FIRST EDITION

10   9   8   7   6   5   4

Dedicated with love to the memory of

my wonderful parents

and to my terrific husband and boys

for the joy they bring me!

CONTENTS

ACKNOWLEDGMENTS

A lot of people gave of themselves for this book to happen. I thank my parents for their love, support, and confidence in me, and for always letting me know that "Yes, I could!" Thank you, Mom, for encouraging this project from an idea through completion. I will always treasure your thumbs-up when the last recipes were written. I appreciate your keeping an eye out for chickens, and I loved watching you play with the boys while I stirred the pot. Thanks, Dad, for your love of the kitchen. It rubbed off.

My wonderful husband, Petrus, and my sweet sons, Blaine and Perrin, I thank you for sharing me with the chickens and for dining on chicken more nights than not. This never could have happened without your sacrifices and your generosity of spirit. Thank you so much, Petrus, for helping me think things through and for battening down the hatches while I cooked and pecked away on the computer. Big thanks, Blaine, for your recipe tips, and Perrin, for helping me put chickens in the grocery cart. Thanks to my sisters, Sharon and Darlene, for their assistance in different ways. It really helped. I appreciate the support from my extended family, including my aunt Dorothy, who sampled recipes. A special thanks to my friend Phyllis, who has been so selfless with her time, her ear, and her thinking cap, which have been helpful in my life and in creating this book. I cannot thank you enough. Thank you, Miki, for your priceless help and your reliability.

I had much appreciated research help from Rachel, Gabrielle, and Sarah. Thanks to my recipe testers: Maria Zebrowski for her superb recipe-testing skills and thoughtfulness, and for cutting many a chicken, and Karen Gillingham and Cathy Hofstetter for a terrific job of helping to wrap up the recipes. Thanks to the many food companies and councils that answered my questions and shared information. Thanks to Ellen Rose of the Cook's Library for allowing me to immerse myself in cookbooks, and to Tim and the staff for their support and knowledge.

Thanks to Jane Dystel of Dystel & Goderich Literary Management for seeing the potential in my concept and to her associate, Stacey Glick, for putting this in front of the right person. A big thanks to the people at Hyperion—the first editor, Jennifer Lang, for bringing the project on board, Natalie Kaire for enthusiastically shepherding it through the process, Will Schwalbe for his expertise, and the behind-the-scenes team that put the book together and got it out to you.

Finally, thank you, the reader, for adding *Rotisserie Chickens to the Rescue!* to your cookbook collection. I appreciate it.

INTRODUCTION

Rotisserie Chickens to the Rescue! was born because I am a time-starved cook who is too stubborn to give up home-cooked meals just because time is tight and my life sometimes borders on chaotic. The concept for this book started with a simple dinner and grew into a quest for letting rotisserie chickens help me do what I have always loved doing: tinkering with recipes, serving myriad different flavors in home-cooked meals, and having the energy to enjoy the meals with everyone else.

My love affair with rotisserie chickens began after I invited friends who were passing through town to come for a spur-of-the-moment weeknight dinner. These friends remembered when I used to mix and roll my own pasta and chop tomatoes to make the sauce. With two young sons and very little time, those days were clearly behind me. As I wandered in the grocery store, children in tow and mumbling to myself about needing another pair of hands, I spotted the case filled with rotisserie chickens. The culinary lightbulb went off. The extra pair of hands was right in that case!

I knew the chickens were tasty because I had bought them on occasion as a take-out alternative for my family. But they were much more than that. Here was a fresh, already-roasted chicken with tender meat just waiting to be used as the base for an even more exciting, more enticing dish. I realized that day that a rotisserie chicken could be used as an *ingredient*. A spice blend here, a quick chop there, and Hurry Curry and my love affair with cooking with rotisserie chickens were born. Dinner was delicious and on time, and I was not the least bit frazzled. My guests wondered how I did it. Since I had known them for so long, I divulged my secret weapon. "It was easy," I replied. "A rotisserie chicken came to my rescue!"

HOT OFF THE ROASTING RACKS

Spit-roasting, the precursor to rotisserie chickens, is one of the oldest methods of cooking. Rotisserie chickens as we know them first cropped up in American supermarkets in the 1950s. Flavored with barbecue seasonings, they puttered along through the '60s, an era when new homes often had built-in ovens with a rotisserie. I still remember my mother proudly inching a freshly roasted chicken off the rod. The National Chicken Council informed me that the trend toward in-store roasting appeared to taper off until the 1990s, and then they moved full-speed ahead. You would be hard-pressed to walk into any supermarket and not find these deliciously convenient and reasonably priced chickens waiting for you. In addition, with rotisserie chickens blooming in popularity, there are the countless chickens roasted at home. Chances are you have a roasted chicken in your refrigerator right now.

NOT "JUST CHICKEN" ANYMORE

In *Rotisserie Chickens to the Rescue!* I share my secrets for transforming a simple rotisserie chicken, store bought or home roasted, or part of a rotisserie chicken, into something different and delicious using readily available ingredients, easy-to-do techniques, and everyday kitchen equipment. These plump, ready-to-eat treasures can be chopped, sliced, or shredded to become a springboard for creating everything from delicious appetizers and sandwiches to tantalizing soups and casseroles, all with very little time and effort—and no special skill required. You can start with a rotisserie chicken and serve everything from Quick Coq au Vin and Chicken and Biscuit Pot Pie to Hot and Sour Soup and Speedy Skillet Paella. Or they can be doused with an easy homemade glaze for an extra-quick flavor boost. You can even cheat a little by warming the whole chicken and surrounding it with a zippy side dish for a presentation you will be proud of.

The recipes in *Rotisserie Chickens to the Rescue!* have the flavor, convenience, and flexibility we look for in cooking and eating. You buy or roast a chicken, open this book, and suddenly you are not serving "just chicken" anymore. Each scrumptious recipe includes the preparation necessary to maximize flavor while minimizing time and effort. I save even more time without sacrificing the good tastes we all crave by taking advantage of the growing bounty of easy-to-use fresh produce, exciting sauces and salsas, and flavorful ethnic ingredients. Never again will you be faced with having to serve a rotisserie chicken plain or tossing out uneaten chicken a few days later. This book will show you that when you have a rotisserie chicken, you have possibilities!

REAL, NOT FANTASY, COOKING

I love food fantasy as much as the next food lover, but my family and I need to eat every day. These recipes reflect that. The recipes in this book are ones that real people can cook within realistic time constraints. A few recipes are a tad more involved—for instance, the Muffaletta Salad requires a fair amount of chopping—but most can be on the table with much less to do. In fact, if a recipe became too involved, I thought about the reality of my life and rethought the recipe because your life is probably as busy as mine, and I want you to use these recipes.

Why These Recipes Will Work for You

One of the things I hope that my book will do is get people in the kitchen cooking, and to do that the recipes must be practical. I use ingredients that are readily available in grocery stores. These recipes were developed, tested, and retested using nonprofessional home ranges because that is what most of you have and I want these recipes to work for you just as I have created them. Professional ranges are much more powerful and can yield different results in different time frames. If you happen to have one, adjust the cooking times as you need to. The only special equipment I used were a food processor in a few recipes and a slow cooker in a smattering of others to take advantage of their convenience.

To help ensure that these recipes will work for you, I used the same safety net that big companies do: I engaged other professional testers to double-check them.

FAMILY FRIENDLY

Feeding a family can be a tricky business. Tight time frames, varied preferences, and multiple schedules can make it challenging to feed a family at home. I have two young sons, and they dined on the recipes in this book. The thumbs-up were many and the thumbs-down few. (I would not expect a six-year-old and a three-year-old to want Muffaletta Salad, but I am all for exposing them to new things.)

I decided not to label recipes that I thought were especially appropriate for children because each child is different. Instead, I worked to develop recipes that would appeal to several age groups, and they have been tasted by everyone from preschoolers to grandmas. Good descriptions and spice recommendations are included to assist you in selecting what is right for your family. You know your family, and you are the best judge of what they will enjoy. I can tell you, though, that they are sure to like the recipes in this book.

HOW TO USE THIS BOOK

There are no secrets to using *Rotisserie Chickens to the Rescue!* It is simple to use. The recipes are straightforward, and the ingredients are easy to find. I have offered tips here and there along with the recipes to make this book even more useful. Among the tips you will find are:

Notes–Tips on ingredients or cooking

Lighter Touch–Ways to reduce fat or calories

In a Pinch–What to do if you are really tight on time or are out of an ingredient

Play It Again–Ideas for using leftovers

These tips and others are there to help make *Rotisserie Chickens to the Rescue!* even more fun and practical to cook from.

WHAT THIS BOOK HOLDS FOR YOU

Rotisserie Chickens to the Rescue! is a treasure trove of more than 125 recipes for the novice and the experienced cook alike. It will put a world of flavors and a full array of easy, delicious options at your fingertips. I hope that you enjoy cooking with *Rotisserie Chickens to the Rescue!* I have certainly enjoyed creating these recipes for you. I am confident that *Rotisserie Chickens to the Rescue!* will be found in your kitchen, not on your bookshelf.

GETTING STARTED

Pantries are indispensable when you are cooking quickly because they give you what you need when you need it. My idea of a pantry includes the cupboard, refrigerator, freezer, and cooking equipment. In this chapter I will show you how to quickly set up what you need to prepare the recipes in this book and how to have what you need at hand. When you do need something at the grocery store, you will often be able to go through the express lane because you will typically not need much to put one of these scrumptious meals on the table.

CONFESSIONS OF A FORMER KITCHEN PACK RAT

I used to have ingredients stockpiled "just in case" and more ingredients stockpiled "just because"— because they looked tasty, because I might use them in a recipe, or because they were on sale. One day, after digging through the cabinet, I surfaced exasperated but jubilant at having found the olives I was searching for. I realized that I had devoted far too much time to the search and wasted precious energy looking for what should have been easy to spot. That ended my stockpiling days.

The purpose of a pantry is *not* to hold everything we might ever need. Its purpose is to put what we are likely to need at our fingertips. After that search for olives, I spent an afternoon going through my cabinets, refrigerator, and freezer and tossing what was outdated. I also lined up like ingredients and jotted down what

I really used. Then I put the most frequently used pots and bowls within easy reach. You may need to spend a few hours, but after you have cleared the decks and bought the provisions for your rotisserie chicken pantry, getting meals together will be faster than ever. Remember, it doesn't matter if you can cook the meal in thirty minutes if it takes you another thirty minutes to find the ingredients and the equipment. Now when I go into the kitchen, I can find what I need when I need it. The olives? They are in the far right row in the cabinet next to the dishwasher.

SHOPPING THE ROTISSERIE CHICKEN WAY

I try to eat before I shop, and I shop with a list. We hear it all the time because it is true: You buy more unnecessary ingredients when you are hungry, and a list saves time and money. I group my list by how the store is set up so I don't end up going back and forth. I also did myself a favor by putting my list on the computer. Now I don't have to handwrite each item every time I go to the store. Create your own shopping list or see pages 8–14 for a sample pantry list.

Once I am in the store, I keep my eyes open, try to stick to the list, and think about what I am planning to cook. I do pay attention to deals, however. If bell peppers are on sale, I might put together my Salsa-Stuffed Bell Peppers with Chipotle Sauce. If I am really pressed for time and am planning the California Cobb Salad for dinner, for example, I might pick up chopped eggs at the salad bar instead of boiling and chopping my own. Already-shredded bagged carrots are available in the produce section, but if I know that I will end up tossing half the bag, I might once again stop by the salad bar and pick up a few handfuls of carrots there. The people in the service deli have even cut rotisserie chickens into serving pieces for me when I had needed them to be ready right away. Thinking outside of the obvious helps me create recipes and get meals to the table with time to spare.

STORING INGREDIENTS THE ROTISSERIE CHICKEN WAY

To keep my cans, bottles, and spices up-to-date, I take a marker and write the purchase date on the label. That way, I use the oldest purchases first and do not end up discarding unused ingredients. Since I now line up ingredients by type, it is a snap to put my hands on what I need and to know when I need more.

I suggest cleaning out your fridge before you go shopping so that you know what you need and can put the groceries away quickly when you get home. Pay attention to what you don't use; you can save yourself space and money by not buying as much the next time. I like to keep things in the same spots all the time in the refrigerator and freezer so that I can find them in a hurry. Hunting for Dijon mustard when preparing Pasta Cordon Bleu or rummaging for frozen mixed vegetables to make Quick Chicken Chowder wastes time and energy. Spare yourself the aggravation by keeping like things together.

FROZEN AND CANNED FOODS

There was a period in the 1980s when "only fresh will do" seemed to be the culinary belief. Frozen packers and canned manufacturers have come a long way in terms of product offerings and we have revised our thinking. Frozen and canned products can offer tasty convenience. Also, some products have other ingredients added, such as chopped peppers in canned corn, offering time-saving flavor. I sometimes use these products to save a step in recipes. Many of the recipes in my book take advantage of frozen and canned vegetables and jarred sauces to create delicious meals in realistic time frames.

Canned cream soups provide a wonderful base for making sauces. If you are watching your fat intake, you can find some reduced-fat cream soups. It is not difficult to make a sauce by blending flour into the pot and stirring in milk or broth. It is faster, however, to open a can of cream soup and pour it into the pot. When all is said and done, the dish is great and the results are fast.

RICE AND PASTAS

The rice aisle today does not even vaguely resemble the rice aisle of old when instant white rice and long-grain white rice were the only choices in the typical supermarket. Now you can find everything from wild rice blends to jasmine rice on shelves everywhere. I am a true rice lover, and I find the wide range of rices available today thrilling. The right rice adds flavor and texture to a meal. Rices cook differently, and I have selected the style of rice that I feel works best for each recipe. For best results I suggest that you stick to that rice—no pun intended.

Our pasta choices are also much broader, with dried and fresh pastas available in a variety of shapes and flavors. I use dried pastas for the recipes in this book because that is what I use at home. They keep well, are less expensive, and are a bit sturdier. If you love fresh pastas, however, and want to experiment with them in a dish, go ahead. I use plain pastas instead of flavored varieties and let the flavors come from the sauces. Asian pastas, from ramen noodles to cellophane and soba noodles, are widely available and offer quick, tasty variety.

SPICES AND DRIED HERBS

You can spend a lot of time looking through the cabinet for herbs and spices. The only thing more frustrating than a long hunt is ending up with an empty bottle. I bought plastic graduated shelves from the hardware store for my herbs and spices, and arranged them in alphabetical order so that I can put my hands on them quickly. Oh, one more thing: I put them back in the slot they came from.

You will notice that with the exception of cilantro, mint, and parsley, I almost always use dried herbs in my recipes. I used to grow many of my own herbs and snip them at will. These days, I find that dried herbs often work best for me. They keep a very long time and are always there when I need them. I don't have time to grow my own anymore, and with dried herbs there is no more tossing out the remnants of bunches that have gone bad because I didn't use them.

Spices are a great way to jump-start the good flavors of rotisserie chicken cooking. Many of my recipes have "spice blend" as the first ingredient. I measure the spices together and mix them up thoroughly so that they will combine well in the dish. This is my way of saving time and making sure that they all get in the pot. Who wants to look up and find the paprika on the counter and the Chicken à la Paprikash headed for the table?

If you make a dish frequently, save yourself even more time. Make multiple batches of the spice blend, store each batch in a small plastic bag, and reach for the blend when you make the dish.

PANTRY LIST

I have put together a list of the ingredients that are helpful to have on hand to prepare the recipes in this book. This is only a guide, of course. If you dislike a particular food, by all means don't buy it. If you love something else, add it to the list. Remember to add an ingredient to your shopping list when your supply is low. Menu planning also helps me keep what I need on hand and within reach. For instance, I always keep a dozen eggs in the fridge, but if I know that I am going to make Cobb Frittata during the week, I will buy the eighteen-egg carton so I will have enough.

This ingredient list will enable you to prepare most of the recipes in this book, but it does not include every ingredient you will need to prepare every recipe in this book because your kitchen would be over-crowded. However, if you use this list as a guideline for setting up your pantry, you will be able to put a great meal on the table.

Long Keepers
CANNED AND JARRED BEANS, FRUITS, NUTS, AND VEGETABLES
Artichoke hearts, marinated and unmarinated
Beans: black, cannelini, garbanzo, kidney, pinto, refried, three-bean salad, Great Northern
Corn: cream style, whole kernel, Mexican style
Mandarin orange segments
Mushrooms, dry
Nuts: slivered almonds, chopped peanuts, peanut butter, walnut pieces
Olives: sliced black, green
Onions, French-fried
Peppers, roasted red
Pimiento, diced
Pineapple in juice: chunks and crushed
Potatoes, sliced
Tomatoes: crushed in purée, diced in juice, paste, sauce, sun-dried (dry or oil-packed)

CONDIMENTS
Capers
Chiles, diced mild
Ketchup
Liquid pepper sauce

Mayonnaise

Mustard, Dijon and regular

Worcestershire sauce

OILS
Extra-virgin olive oil

Nonstick cooking spray

Vegetable oil

RICE, PASTA, AND GRAINS
Couscous, instant plain

Pasta, dried: alphabet, fettuccine, small elbow macaroni, penne, spaghetti, wide egg noodles

Polenta: 24- to 28-ounce tube

Ramen noodles, chicken flavored

Rice: extra-long white, instant brown, instant white, jasmine, yellow

Stuffing mix: chicken flavored, cornbread

SAUCES AND DRESSINGS
Alfredo sauce, jarred

Barbecue sauce

Pasta sauce or spaghetti sauce

Salad dressings of choice, clear and creamy

Salsa: chunky, green, and regular

Soy sauce, regular and lite

Stir-fry sauce

Sweet-and-sour sauce

Teriyaki sauce

DRIED HERBS, SPICES, AND SEASONINGS

Ground herbs and spices can be stored for at least six months if kept in a cool, dry, dark place, like a cabinet. Open the bottles and give the spices a quick whiff. If they smell like the spice, they are good. Otherwise, toss them and replace them. Listings with an asterisk (*) are used in one or two recipes.

Allspice, ground

Basil leaves

Bay leaves

Chili powder

Cinnamon, ground

*Creole seasoning

Cumin, ground and seed

Curry powder

Dill weed

*Fajita seasoning

*Garam masala

Garlic powder

Ginger, ground

*Greek seasoning

Italian herb seasoning

Mustard, dry

Nutmeg, ground

*Old Bay seasoning

Onion powder

Oregano

Paprika

Parsley flakes

Pepper: black, cayenne, red pepper flakes, white

*Pumpkin pie seasoning

Rosemary

Salt

Thyme

Chicken broth: fat-free less-sodium, about ten 14$\frac{1}{2}$-ounce cans

Corn muffin mix

Cornstarch

Croutons: garlic and herb

Garlic, jarred minced (typically found in produce section)

Ginger, jarred chopped (typically found in produce section)

Flour

Milk: canned evaporated and unsweetened coconut

Raisins

Soups: Cheddar cheese, cream of broccoli, cream of chicken, cream of mushroom, cream of potato, tomato

Sweeteners: brown sugar, granulated sugar, honey

Taco shells: regular size, ready-to-eat

Tortilla chips

WINE AND VINEGAR

Vinegar: cider, unseasoned rice, red wine

Wine: dry white or dry vermouth

Quickly Perishable, and Refrigerated and Frozen

BREAD

Biscuits, refrigerated—large-size buttermilk

French sandwich rolls: 6-inch (can be wrapped and frozen)

Pita rounds (can be wrapped and frozen)

Prebaked pizza crust: 12-inch (can be frozen)

Tortillas: taco-size corn and burrito-size flour

DAIRY AND EGGS

Butter

Cheeses

- Already-shredded: mild Cheddar, sharp Cheddar, Italian blend, Monterey Jack, mozzarella, Parmesan
- Cream: reduced-fat and whipped
- Feta
- Parmesan: grated

Eggs, large

Half-and-half

Milk

Sour cream: light

Yogurt, plain

FRESH FRUITS, HERBS, AND VEGETABLES

Tart apples, such as Granny Smith and Pippin (ask your produce person for good tart apples in your area)

Bananas

Bell peppers: green and red

Broccoli florets

Carrots: already-shredded, baby, whole

Cilantro

Coleslaw mix

Lemons, two

Limes, three

Mushrooms, sliced

Onions: green, red, and yellow (large, not the new jumbo variety)

Parsley: flat-leaf (Italian)

Potatoes: red, russet

Salad greens: already-torn, prewashed, and ready-to-eat

Shallots

Tomatoes, cherry and regular

FROZEN FRUITS AND VEGETABLES

Beans: green, lima

Broccoli: chopped, and in cheese sauce

Corn kernels

Mixed vegetables

Onions, pearl

Orange juice concentrate

Peas and carrots

Spinach: chopped, and creamed

MEAT, POULTRY, AND SEAFOOD

Bacon: one pound, wrapped four slices to a pack and frozen

Rotisserie chicken pieces

Rotisserie chicken carcasses (in freezer if you like to make stock)

Sausage, smoked: andouille and kielbasa (can be frozen)

Shrimp: about 100 per pound (bought and stored frozen)

EQUIPMENT

I am not a gadget cook, and this is not a fancy-equipment cookbook. My rescue recipes use only basic, easy-to-use, easy-to-wash equipment. You can prepare all but a handful of the recipes in this book if you have the following basic equipment:

- Good chef's knife (I use an 8-inch for everyday cooking)
- Heavy-bottomed 12-inch nonstick skillet with deep sides
- Soup pot (I use an 8-quart)

- Dutch oven
- 8 × 8-inch glass baking pan
- 13 × 9-inch glass baking pan
- Baking sheet
- 2-quart saucepan
- 3-quart saucepan

I round out the big equipment with this short list of small equipment:

- Rubber spatula for mixing and stirring in the bowl
- Large non-metal heat resistant spoon
- Large non-metal heat-resistant slotted spoon
- Wooden spoon(s)
- Non-metal spatula for turning food on the stove
- Wire cooling rack
- Colander
- Wire whisk
- Mixing bowls
- Cutting board

How to Select and Care for Equipment

Not all pots and pans are created equal. Pots and pans made of different materials can wear and conduct heat differently. I prefer stainless steel and enameled cast iron because they cook evenly and do not react with food. I find that heavier pans conduct heat more efficiently and evenly, and they last longer. Look for a heavy nonstick skillet with a handle that is oven safe up to at least 350° F. The handle will be a big help when a recipe goes from stovetop to skillet.

Caring for pots and pans properly can make them last much longer. Follow the manufacturer's instructions for using, cleaning, and storing. Never use a metal turner or spoon with a nonstick skillet. And if you need to stack a nonstick skillet in a cabinet, put a tea towel on top of the nonstick finish to protect it before putting another pan inside.

How to Store Equipment

One of my pet peeves in the kitchen is having to dig out equipment. I keep my trusty 12-inch nonstick skillet and my saucepans on top of the stove. My Dutch oven and soup pot are in the front of the cabinet so that I can get them quickly and not waste precious time moving things around. Keep the utensils and equipment that you use frequently within easy reach. I keep my favorite spatulas and spoons in a little holder on the counter next to the stove so they are where I need them when I need them.

CHICKEN PICKING

Rotisserie chickens are everywhere, and selecting a chicken is fairly effortless. There is no need to stand over the case and ruminate. I buy chickens in a variety of places, from my local warehouse store to the neighborhood supermarket. I have used chickens from all these stores in my recipes, and they all worked well. Below are some quick guidelines that I hope you will find useful in buying, storing, and cutting rotisserie chickens.

CHICKEN FLAVORS

Rotisserie chickens come in a variety of flavors, ranging from plain unsalted and barbecue to lemon herb. Most of the flavor from the seasoning tends to be in the skin, so you do not have to worry about the seasoning when choosing a chicken. If you do not want that flavor, simply peel away the skin. If you know what recipe you are going to prepare, however, go ahead and select a chicken flavor that is compatible.

BUYING AND STORING CHICKENS

Rotisserie chickens are so readily available that the United States Department of Agriculture has issued safety guidelines for selecting them and storing them. They advise you to follow the old food safety adage "Keep hot food hot and cold food cold" when picking a chicken. The chicken should be hot when you buy it. Bacteria become active between 40° and 140° F. so the chicken should be above that range when you buy it. Remember, body temperature is just under 99° F., so the chicken case and package should feel pretty warm to the touch.

Since the chickens should be hot, I suggest that you pick them up at the end of your shopping trip, like all temperature-sensitive food. You should either eat or refrigerate the chicken within two hours to help keep it safe. You should try to eat or refrigerate it more quickly in hot weather. Ideally, if you are going to refrigerate it, you should cut it into serving pieces and store, uncovered, in a shallow container to help it cool down quickly, covering the container when the chicken cools down. You can also shred it or chop it for a recipe and refrigerate the pieces.

BUY TWO ROTISSERIE CHICKENS

If you buy two, you can cook with one today and cook with one tomorrow or the next day. The USDA recommends eating rotisserie chickens within three to four days of purchase, and it is safe to eat it cold or reheated up to 165° F. At that temperature the chicken would be hot. If you find that you are not going to use the entire chicken within three or four days, freeze the unused pieces in a good-quality freezer bag and use them within four months. Thaw the chicken in the refrigerator or the microwave, not on the counter-top. I use rotisserie chicken that has been frozen in dishes that are cooked rather than in salads or sand-wiches.

THE SIZE OF THE CHICKEN

Just as uncooked chickens are different sizes, rotisserie chickens are different sizes. Some stores sell them by the pound, and you pick the size you want. Others sell them by the chicken and standardize their size. Some chains even offer two different sizes: a premium size and a smaller, regular size. An average 32-ounce rotisserie chicken will give you about 3–3½ cups of chicken meat. One warehouse store in my area has chickens with very large breasts, and they have more meat overall. If you experiment with the chickens in your area, you will discover any preferences and then be able to shop accordingly. Each recipe in this book has been tested with chickens from two different stores, and they all worked just fine.

GETTING TO THE MEAT OF THE MATTER: CUTTING THE CHICKEN

One of the many joys of cooking with rotisserie chickens—in addition to not having to go through the rigors of cleaning up after handling raw chicken—is that it is much easier to cut a cooked chicken than a raw one and to get the meat off the bone. My recipes use chicken meat in several forms: still on the bone, sliced, chopped, shredded, and pulled into chunks. The way to start is by cutting the chicken into serving pieces. This is my primer on how you quickly get to each type of meat.

First, I always put a damp paper towel under the cutting board to keep it from moving around. The next question is: skin on or skin off? It is important for some recipes that the skin be removed, and I have noted that in those recipes. In most of the recipes it is largely a matter of taste, so I leave it up to you to decide. If you are going to remove the skin, simply peel it off before you cut, shred, or pull the meat into chunks.

Cutting the Chicken into Pieces

No need to fret. This is very easy. The only secret to cutting a chicken is feeling for where the bones attach to the body and to one another. Once you do that, cutting is a breeze. Follow these easy steps, and you will have no trouble.

- Put the chicken on the cutting board, breast side up, and pull out your sharp chef's knife.
- To separate the wings from the chicken, cut along where the wing attaches to the breast.
- Feel for where the thighs connect to the breast and cut the thighs and legs off. The thighs should come off easily.
- Put the leg and thigh on the cutting board with the underside facing up. Put your finger where the thigh and leg connect and wiggle your finger into the joint. This is where you cut to separate the thigh from the leg. Cut the leg from the thigh.

- The breasts are the only pieces left on the chicken at this point. If you want to slice the chicken for a sandwich, start at the top of the breast, slice thinly down and parallel to the bone to remove the meat, working your way from the outside of the chicken in.

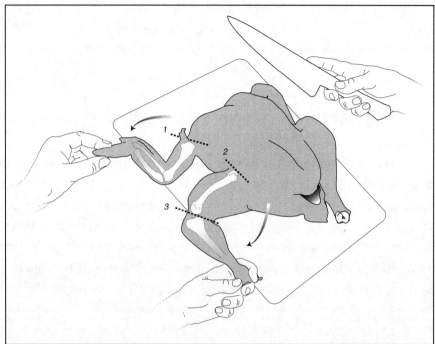

If you want to remove each breast half in one piece because you need slivers, chunks, thick slices, or simply prefer slicing that way, feel for where the meat attaches to the chicken and cut along where the meat attaches to the chicken. Take your time. You are not carving the Thanksgiving turkey and all eyes are not on you. This is simple. Now you can remove the breast pieces whole. Put the breast skin side up on the cutting board and cut slices, slivers, or cubes, as needed.

- You now have the carcass. You can use it, freeze it, or discard it. If you are shredding the meat for the recipe and are not using the carcass, be sure to pull any remaining meat from it.

Cutting the Meat into Chunks

When a recipe calls for bite-size chunks, cut the chicken into about ½-inch cubes. Hold the drumsticks up by the bone and slice down to remove the meat, cutting on all four sides. Lay the meat flat on the cutting

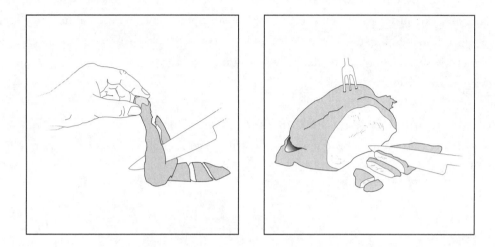

board and cut lengthwise and then crosswise to cut into the desired size pieces. You can slice meat from the drummette (the fat part of the wing) by cutting just as you did for the drumstick. You cannot slice meat from the other part of the wing, so you will have to eat it. To get the meat off the thighs, cut along the bones and then cut into pieces as for the drumsticks. For the breast, cut along the grain and then cut crosswise into the desired size cubes.

TO CUT OR NOT TO CUT

I have shredded and hand-chunked so many rotisserie chickens that when I want this type of meat, I often pull the chicken into serving pieces rather than cut them since I do not need clean cuts. The choice is yours.

To pull into shreds:

There is something so nice and tender about shreds of rotisserie chicken, and they are wonderfully easy to get to. I use two types of shreds in my recipes: fine and large. Fine shreds just means that each piece of meat is pulled into more pieces. To shred the meat, cut or pull the chicken into serving pieces. Then pull pieces of meat off the bone by hand. Use your fingers to pull the meat into shreds, pulling along the grain or lines of the meat. If you are pulling along the grain, the meat will come apart very easily.

Precise sizes of chicken pieces are not key to these recipes. The dimensions I give here are mere guidelines. By all means, do not measure to make shreds. Use your judgment and eyeball it. In my recipes, fine shreds are about 1½-inches long by ¼-inch wide and ¼-inch or so thick. Large shreds are about 1½-inches long by ½-inch wide and ½-inch or so thick. These measurements are approximate, just to give you an idea of the size range you are looking for.

To pull the meat into large chunks:

Once you have cut or pulled the chicken into serving pieces, simply pull along the grain to make large chunks, about 1½-inches long by ½-inch wide by ½-inch deep.

QUICK STARTS

Homemade appetizers are one of life's simple pleasures. As a start to a meal, a little something to nibble on while relaxing with family or friends, or center stage for a buffet, a good appetizer brings with it the promise of more delicious bites and fun to come. Deli counters and freezer cases are filled with ready-to-serve morsels, but as hectic as life is, I refuse to give up that special feeling that comes from preparing my own sometimes. The recipes in this chapter are proof that delicious does not have to be difficult or time-consuming. When you start with a plump rotisserie chicken, you can serve everything from casual Eight-Layer Dip with Spicy Chicken to more elegant Stuffed Mushrooms Alfredo with a minimum of time and effort.

Appetizers should be fast and fun. Who has time to spend endless hours fussing over little gems and arranging them just so on a platter? When you choose from this selection, you have exciting flavors that can quickly offer something scrumptious to nibble on while chatting, sipping a cool drink, or anticipating a main course. Many of the recipes can be prepared ahead of time, and tips are included for even easier serving.

Remember these delectable bites for a special occasion or make an everyday occasion special by reaching for the rotisserie chicken to start things off just right. With the time you save, you may even have a few minutes to fuss with how they look on the platter.

STUFFED MUSHROOMS ALFREDO

–Makes about eighteen 2-inch caps–

A rotisserie chicken, ready-to-serve Alfredo sauce, and already-seasoned Italian bread crumbs make short order of these luscious little delicacies. This recipe doubles well and is perfect pre-dinner or buffet fare. Delicious with a glass of white wine or sparkling cider, these mushrooms are easy to serve since you can bake them a few hours ahead and refrigerate. To reheat, put a little water, chicken broth, or white wine in the bottom of a pan and microwave or heat in a 350° F. oven.

18 large mushrooms (about 2 inches across), stems removed and reserved for another use
Olive oil
1½ cups finely shredded rotisserie chicken, skin removed and meat pulled apart by hand
⅔ cup refrigerated Alfredo sauce, not reduced-fat
½ cup packaged seasoned dry Italian bread crumbs

¼ cup finely chopped onion (about ½ small onion)
2 tablespoons finely chopped flat-leaf (Italian) parsley
1 teaspoon jarred minced garlic
Salt and pepper, to taste
1 egg, beaten
¼ cup already-shredded Parmesan cheese

1. Preheat the oven to 350° F. Lightly brush or drizzle the insides and outsides of the mushroom caps with the oil. Place on a baking sheet with edges or in a 13 × 9-inch pan.

2. Mix the chicken, Alfredo sauce, bread crumbs, onion, parsley, and garlic together in a medium bowl. Season with salt and pepper. Mix in the egg. Mound about 1 rounded tablespoon of the filling mixture in each of the caps, pressing down firmly and forming a dome in the center. Sprinkle with the cheese.

3. Bake until the filling is firm to the touch, 20–25 minutes. Serve warm or at room temperature.

▶ Notes

- Select mushroom caps close to the same size for even baking.
- A serrated grapefruit spoon works well for hollowing out the mushrooms.
- To save even more time, buy already-chopped onions in the produce section and just chop them a little more finely.
- For an extra touch of elegance, pour about 1 cup of white wine into a 13 × 9-inch baking pan. Add the stuffed mushrooms and bake as directed.

Play It Again: Save the mushroom stems to add to soup or to toss on a quick salad.

Do-Ahead Tip: Hollow out the mushrooms a day in advance, cover lightly with foil, and refrigerate.

Double Duty: This recipe doubles well.

HOISIN LETTUCE ROLLS

—Makes 12 pieces—

These no-cook bundles are the perfect choice when you are playing beat-the-clock but want an enticing start to a meal. Sweet and spicy at the same time, hoisin sauce, also called Peking sauce, is a mainstay of Chinese cooking. Look for it in the Asian section of the supermarket. If you buy it in a jar, once opened it will keep for two to three months in the refrigerator.

2 cups finely chopped rotisserie chicken, skin removed
½ cup hoisin sauce, plus additional for dipping
3 medium green onions, thinly sliced (about ½ cup)

1 small tart apple, unpeeled and finely chopped (about ½ cup)
1½ teaspoons rice vinegar, unseasoned
½ cup chopped walnuts
12 Boston lettuce leaves, washed and dried

1. Stir the chicken, ¼ cup hoisin sauce, onions, apple, rice vinegar, and walnuts together in a medium bowl. Spoon about ¼ cup of the chicken mixture in the center of a lettuce leaf, leaving a 1-inch border on each side. Roll into a cylinder. Repeat with the remaining leaves. Serve, seam side down, with additional hoisin sauce for dipping if desired.

> **Do-Ahead Tip:** You can wash and dry the lettuce leaves a day ahead. Put the dry leaves between slightly damp paper towels, seal them in a plastic bag, and tuck them in the crisper.

Serve It Up: Show off the filling for a different and pretty presentation. Simply scoop the chicken mixture in the center of the lettuce leaves and arrange the open leaves on a platter.

Double Duty: This recipe doubles well.

ROASTED CHICKEN AND DILL SLATHER

—Makes about 1½ cups—

This delightful appetizer goes together in a snap, making it a good choice when guests are coming and time is very short. It is so fast to prepare that you might even find yourself treating your family to an unexpected pre-dinner treat when you need a little pick-me-up. This can be refrigerated for two days if you make it with a chicken roasted that day.

2 (3-ounce) packages cream cheese, at room temperature

1 cup chopped rotisserie chicken breast, skin removed

2 tablespoons sliced green onions, white part only (about 3 medium onions)

2 tablespoons fresh dill leaves or 1 teaspoon dried

2½ teaspoons freshly-squeezed lemon juice

¼ teaspoon salt

¼ teaspoon white pepper

Crackers, toasted baguette slices, or celery sticks

1. Cut the cream cheese into cubes. Place in the bowl of a food processor and process until creamy. Scrape down the sides. Add the chicken, onions, dill, lemon juice, salt, and pepper. Process until the mixture is smooth, scraping down the sides as needed.

2. Spoon into a bowl. Cover well and chill until ready to serve. Serve with crackers, baguette slices, or celery.

VARIATION

Roasted Chicken, Dill, and Caper Slather:

Omit the salt and stir in 1 tablespoon of drained capers after removing the mixture from the processor.

▶ Notes

- If you have an 8-ounce package of cream cheese, cut it in half crosswise, then cut each half in half to form four pieces. Use three of the pieces for the recipe and save the last one for another use.
- For fresh dill leaves in a hurry, hold the dill branch at the top and run your fingers down the stem. The delicate leaves will come right off.

Lighter Touch: Reduced-fat cream cheese works quite well in this recipe.

Play It Again: Spread leftovers on a toasted bagel and top with tomato slices for a great lunch in a hurry.

FETA AND BASIL CROSTINI

—Makes about 30 pieces—

Heady with garlic and the rich tanginess of the classic Greek feta cheese, these party pleasers are a sophisticated marriage of grilled cheese sandwiches and garlic toast. They are intended to be little bites, so look for a slender baguette instead of the big, fluffy loaves you would use for a submarine sandwich. You can save a few steps if the deli section of your grocery store has baked garlic toasts or crostini in bags.

TOASTS

1 slender baguette (about 8 ounces), sliced diagonally (about ½-inch thick)
3 tablespoons olive oil
2 large cloves garlic, cut in half

TOPPING

1¼ cup crumbled feta cheese (about 5 ounces)
1 cup finely shredded skinless rotisserie chicken, skin removed and meat pulled apart by hand
¼ cup finely chopped fresh basil leaves

1 cup chopped tomatoes and their juice (about 2 medium tomatoes)
White pepper, to taste
Olive oil for drizzling (about 2 tablespoons)
Fresh basil leaves for garnish

1. **MAKE THE TOASTS:** Position two racks in the oven: one at the bottom and one in the center. Preheat the oven to 350° F. Place the baguette slices on baking sheets and brush with the oil. Bake until the slices are slightly firm to the touch and the edges are light brown, about 8 minutes. Switch the sheets from top to bottom after about 5 minutes. Slide the slices onto a flat surface. Spear a cut garlic clove with a fork and rub the light brown side of the slices with

the garlic. Use a new clove about one-fourth of the way through the slices. Move a rack to about 4 inches from the broiler. Change the oven heat to broil.

2. **MAKE THE TOPPING:** Mix the feta, chicken, and basil together in a small bowl. Gently stir in the tomatoes and juice. Add the pepper.

3. Mound about 2 teaspoons of the feta mixture on the garlic-rubbed side of each slice of toast, pressing down slightly. Drizzle a little oil over the center of each slice. Return the slices to the baking sheets and broil until the topping is hot and the cheese begins to melt, 1–2 minutes.

4. Place on a platter and garnish with basil leaves. Serve immediately.

▶ Notes

- A serrated knife is the best tool for slicing a baguette. Cut one slice and use it as a guide for the others.
- After chopping the tomatoes, place the measuring cup under the cutting board and use a rubber spatula to scoop both the tomatoes and their juice into the cup.
- To keep basil bright green, wash it just before using and pat it dry gently. Chop it with a very sharp knife to avoid discoloring bruises.

Do-Ahead Tip: The toasts can be baked a day ahead and stored at room temperature in an airtight container with a lid. Make the filling the day of the party.

Lighter Touch: If you are watching your weight, spray the slices with olive oil spray instead of brushing them with olive oil.

Double Duty: This recipe doubles well.

HOT ARTICHOKE AND CHICKEN DIP

—Makes about 4 cups—

My rotisserie chicken version of the ever popular crab dip can be on your table in minutes. Serve this in a chafing dish or even in a slow cooker on low for a great open-house or potluck choice. For a more dramatic look, hollow out the center of a sturdy round loaf of bread and spoon the hot dip into the middle.

DIP

1 (8-ounce) package reduced-fat cream cheese, cut into 8 cubes

1 (4-ounce) container garlic and herb cheese spread

1½ cups shredded rotisserie chicken, skin removed and meat pulled apart by hand

1 (14-ounce) can unmarinated artichoke hearts, drained and chopped

1 cup shredded Swiss cheese

½ cup mayonnaise

1 tablespoon Dijon mustard

1 teaspoon paprika

¼ teaspoon salt

ACCOMPANIMENTS

Assortment of crackers, celery and carrot sticks

1. **MAKE THE DIP:** Combine the dip ingredients in a large microwaveable bowl, stirring well. Microwave, covered, on high power until hot and the cheeses are melted, about 3 minutes. Stir well and serve with accompaniments.

▶ Note
   • Pick up ready-to-serve celery and carrot sticks in the produce section.

IRRESISTIBLE DEVILED EGGS

—Makes 12 pieces—

I have always been a lover of deviled eggs, and these have a generous amount of filling. The connection between the chicken and the egg comes right through in the taste of this quicker-than-quick appetizer. They travel well, making them great for picnics. Once the eggs are boiled and the onions are sliced, you can turn this over to the kids, who will be happy to mash, stir, and spoon the filling. Our sons are equally as happy to eat them.

SPICE BLEND

½ teaspoon garlic powder
¼ teaspoon salt
Pinch of white pepper

FILLING

6 large hard-cooked eggs, peeled
1 cup finely chopped rotisserie chicken
¼ cup Dijon mustard
3 tablespoons thinly sliced green onion

2 tablespoons mayonnaise
2 tablespoons jarred diced pimentos
1 teaspoon freshly-squeezed lemon juice

1. **MAKE THE SPICE BLEND:** Stir the ingredients together in a small bowl and set aside.

2. **MAKE THE FILLING:** Slice the eggs in half lengthwise. Scoop the yolks into a medium-size mixing bowl. Mash the yolks with a fork until there are no lumps. Add the chicken, mustard, onion, mayonnaise, pimentos, and lemon juice, along with the spice blend. Stir well. Spoon into the center of the egg whites, mounding a generous amount of filling in each egg. Serve immediately or refrigerate, covered, until serving time.

CRUNCHY CHEESY CHICKEN NACHOS

*_Makes about 8–10 servings_*

Americans have a love affair with nachos. A blanket of cheese on top keeps the chunks of roasted chicken moist and tender, and also adds that "ooze" factor we all think of with nachos. Be sure to use mild cheese. Sharp does not melt as well here, and I find the flavor overpowering. The jalapeños are classic and the onions add a nice bite.

1 (12 to 16-ounce) bag tortilla chips
2 cups bite-size chunks rotisserie chicken, skin removed
About 4 cups already-shredded mild Cheddar cheese

4 green onions, thinly sliced
Sliced jalapeños packed in vinegar, drained
½ cup chopped cilantro (optional)

ACCOMPANIMENTS

Sour cream
Prepared salsa
Prepared guacamole

1. Position a rack in the top of the oven. Preheat the oven to 400° F. Line a 15 × 13-inch baking sheet with foil, shiny side down.

2. Cover the baking sheet with a single layer of slightly overlapping chips. You will need about a generous 9 cups for this size sheet. Scatter the chicken on the chips and then the cheese. Sprinkle with the onions and dot with jalapeños, as desired. Bake until the cheese is bubbly and melted, about 10 minutes. Sprinkle with the cilantro, if desired. Use a wide spatula to transfer to a serving platter and serve with the accompaniments.

VARIATION

Black Bean and Chicken Nachos:

Rinse and drain one 15-ounce can of black beans. Sprinkle the beans on the tortilla chips, followed by the chicken, cheese, onions, and jalapeños, in that order. Bake as directed above.

▶ ## Note

- How many chips you need depends on the size of the baking sheet. If your sheet is smaller than mine, you can bake two batches or cut the recipe in half and bake one sheet. How much cheese you use is a matter of preference.

MEDITERRANEAN PARTY PLATTER
WITH ROASTED PEPPER HUMMUS

—Makes about 2 cups of hummus—

Roasted chicken adds a subtle richness to this tangy take on hummus. It is the perfect colorful center for a party platter. Surround the flavorful hummus with mounds of pita wedges, crackers, ready-to-eat jars of marinated vegetables from your pantry, and romaine lettuce from your crisper for a party in no time. Be creative with your offerings and select the mix and quantities that work for you. Chock-full of good-for-you legumes and vegetables, this is guilt-free entertaining at its delicious best.

SPICE BLEND

2 teaspoons ground cumin
1 teaspoon dried rosemary, crumbled between the fingers

½ teaspoon salt

HUMMUS

¾ cup rinsed and drained canned garbanzo beans (a generous one-third of a 15-ounce can)
4 teaspoons freshly-squeezed lemon juice
1 tablespoon jarred minced garlic
1 tablespoon olive oil
1 cup firmly packed chopped rotisserie chicken breast, skin removed

¼ cup firmly packed flat-leaf (Italian) parsley leaves
¼ cup chopped onion (about ½ small onion)
⅓ cup chopped jarred roasted red pepper plus ½ cup finely chopped jarred roasted red pepper
¼ cup coarsely chopped sun-dried tomatoes, oil-packed or dry and rehydrated
Parsley sprigs for garnish (optional)

ACCOMPANIMENTS

Pita bread cut into wedges, crackers

Kalamata olives

Torn chilled romaine lettuce leaves

Marinated vegetables: artichoke hearts, mushrooms, pearl onions, and green beans

1. **MAKE THE SPICE BLEND:** Stir the ingredients together in a small bowl and set aside.

2. **MAKE THE HUMMUS:** Place the garbanzo beans, lemon juice, garlic, oil, and spice blend in the bowl of a food processor and process until smooth. Scrape down the sides as needed. Add the chicken and parsley, and continue to process until the mixture sticks together and forms balls.

3. Add the onion, the $1/3$ cup red pepper, and the sun-dried tomatoes and process until smooth. Scrape down the sides as needed. Scoop the mixture into a serving bowl, stir in the $1/2$ cup finely chopped red pepper, and season with pepper. Garnish with parsley sprigs if desired. Serve with accompaniments.

▶ Note

- If you have fresh green beans on hand, cook them just until crisp-tender and serve them instead of the marinated green beans.

Do-Ahead Tip: The hummus can be made a day ahead, covered, and refrigerated.

Feeling Flush: If you have the time, home-toasted pita crisps are just great. Preheat the oven to 350° F. Stir 2 teaspoons jarred minced garlic into 2 tablespoons olive oil. Cut pita rounds into wedges and place on baking sheets. Brush lightly with the oil or lightly coat with garlic spray. Bake until crisp but not hard, 8–10 minutes.

Serve It Up: This is perfect potluck or office party fare. Spoon the hummus into a heavy-duty plastic bag and pack the veggies in individual plastic bags. Add the pita and crackers, a platter, and a bowl, and you are ready to take your show on the road.

Play It Again: Toss leftover vegetables with chunks of rotisserie chicken for a great salad topper. No dressing is needed since the veggies are marinated.

EIGHT-LAYER DIP WITH SPICY CHICKEN

—Makes about 12 servings—

This quick, hearty dip is a party in a dish. A glass pan shows off the dip's pretty layers. If you do not have one, make the dip anyway; it will be just as tasty. The contrast of textures, flavors, and colors makes this fun food you will serve again and again. If you add a bowl of sturdy tortilla chips and nice cold drinks, you just might hear cries of "Olé!"

SPICE BLEND

2 teaspoons chili powder

2 teaspoons ground cumin

1½ teaspoons dried oregano, crumbled
between the fingers

1 teaspoon garlic powder

DIP LAYERS

1 (16-ounce) jar chunky salsa (about 2 cups),
at room temperature

1 (16-ounce) can refried beans

1 (4-ounce) can diced mild chiles, drained

3 green onions, thinly sliced (about ½ cup)

1 (8-ounce) container light sour cream
(about 1 cup), at room temperature

1 (3.8-ounce) can sliced black olives, drained

2 cups bite-size chunks rotisserie chicken, skin
removed and meat pulled apart by hand

1 (8-ounce) container prepared guacamole

Already-shredded Mexican blend cheese,
to taste

Sturdy tortilla chips

1. **MAKE THE SPICE BLEND:** Stir the ingredients together in a medium bowl and set aside.

2. **MAKE THE LAYERED DIP:** Put a strainer over a measuring cup and pour the salsa in to drain while you assemble the dip. Drain until no liquid remains in the salsa, stirring frequently

to help remove the liquid. Work in batches if necessary. Scoop the salsa pieces into a bowl and reserve the liquid.

3. Spoon the beans into a small bowl and stir in the chiles. Spread over the bottom of an 8 × 8 × 2-inch glass baking dish. Sprinkle the onions over the beans, forming a second layer.

4. Stir the sour cream to make it easier to spread and spoon it over the onions. Gently spread it to the edges of the baking dish, trying not to mix the onion in. Sprinkle the olives over the sour cream. You will now have 4 layers.

5. Add the chicken and 2 tablespoons of the reserved salsa liquid to the spice blend. Stir well to thoroughly coat the chicken with the spices. Sprinkle the chicken over the olives. Add the drained salsa to the pan and spread to the edges of the pan. Then carefully spread the guacamole over the salsa. You will now have 7 layers.

6. Sprinkle cheese, as desired, over all. This is layer 8. Serve with the tortilla chips.

▶ Notes
- Do not skip or rush the draining step; if you do, the salsa will be too liquidy.
- Try refried black beans for a deeper, smokier flavor.

Company's Coming: You can put this together after guests arrive. It also travels quite well to potlucks.

Play It Again: For a quick burrito lunch or dinner, warm any leftovers and wrap in steaming hot tortillas warmed in the microwave according to package directions. Serve a green salad alongside.

In a Pinch: If time is truly short, substitute refried beans already seasoned with peppers and onions for the plain refried beans and diced chiles.

Double Duty: This recipe doubles well. Use a 13×9-inch pan.

Lighter Touch: Fat-free beans and light sour cream work just fine.

SPICE ISLAND TURNOVERS WITH
PINEAPPLE MANGO DIPPING SAUCE

—Makes about twenty-eight 2¾ to 3-inch turnovers—

Fragrant with cinnamon and cloves, these tropical turnovers were inspired by the wonderful bounty of fresh spices that grow on the tiny Caribbean island of Grenada, the Spice Island, and the region's love of meat-stuffed pastries. These delectable morsels are bursting with golden raisins and tender chicken, and the quick tropical dipping sauce gilds the lily. These are the most time-consuming appetizer in this chapter, but one bite reveals that they are worth every minute.

FILLING

1 cup finely chopped rotisserie chicken
1 (4-ounce) jar diced pimientos, drained (about ½ cup)
⅓ cup finely chopped red onion (about ½ small onion)
⅓ cup golden raisins

2 tablespoons frozen orange juice concentrate, thawed
1 tablespoon water
1½ teaspoons pumpkin pie spice
1 teaspoon jarred minced garlic
¼ teaspoon salt

CRUST

2 (15-ounce) packages refrigerated piecrust, at room temperature
Flour

1 egg, beaten with a pinch salt and 1 tablespoon milk or water

Pineapple Mango Dipping Sauce (recipe follows)

1. **MAKE THE FILLING:** Stir the ingredients together in a medium bowl. Set aside.

2. **PREPARE THE CRUST:** Position one rack in the bottom of the oven and another rack in the middle. Preheat the oven to 350° F. Line two baking sheets with parchment paper or aluminum foil. Place one piecrust on a lightly floured work surface, pressing the dough down gently to flatten the crease. Dip a 2¾- to 3-inch round cookie cutter or glass in the flour and cut circles from the dough, starting in the center and working out to the edge. Repeat with the remaining dough until you have cut 28 circles. Store any unused dough according to package directions.

3. Flip the circles over and place 1 rounded teaspoon of the filling in the center of each circle. Do not overfill. Wet the inside edges with water. Fold in half, stretching gently if necessary. Do not tear the crust. Press the edges together gently to seal, then press the tines of a fork firmly along the seal.

4. Position the filled turnovers 2 inches apart on the prepared baking sheets and brush lightly with the beaten egg mixture. Bake until golden brown, 15 to 20 minutes, reversing the sheets top to bottom after about 10 minutes. Transfer to wire racks to cool slightly.

5. Make the Pineapple Mango Dipping Sauce while the turnovers are baking. Serve the turnovers warm with the Pineapple Mango Dipping Sauce.

PINEAPPLE MANGO DIPPING SAUCE

Makes about 1¼ cups

1 (8-ounce) can crushed pineapple in its own juice, drained
½ cup Major Grey's mango chutney
3 tablespoons frozen orange juice concentrate, thawed

1. Place the pineapple, chutney, and orange juice concentrate in a food processor or blender. Process until combined and almost smooth.

Do-Ahead Tips
- Place the unbaked turnovers on a baking sheet and freeze. Remove from the baking sheet, pop into a freezer bag, and store for up to two weeks. To bake, thaw in a single layer in the refrigerator overnight and bake as directed in the recipe.
- When piecrusts are on sale, buy several and cut a supply of these rounds. Freeze with waxed paper between the rounds.
- You can make the sauce a day ahead. Let it come to room temperature before serving or warm it slightly in the microwave.

Turnover Tips: Refrigerated piecrust makes easy work of these homemade turnovers. There is nothing tricky about making a good turnover; just fill and seal them properly. To succeed every time, remember:
- More filling is not better. Do not overfill them, or they will burst open in the oven.
- Seal firmly all the way around so that the edges stay together in the oven.

Double Duty: This recipe doubles well.

Feeling Flush: Substitute ¾ teaspoon ground cinnamon, ½ teaspoon ground allspice, and ¼ teaspoon ground cloves for the pumpkin pie spice.

STANDOUT SALADS

If you are a salad lover, you will love this chapter. If you are not, watch out—these recipes are likely to convert you. You can enjoy main dish salads very quickly when you have a rotisserie chicken. Our supermarkets are bursting with a full array of delicious vinegars, sauces, dressings, grains, and produce that you can combine with a rotisserie chicken to make a standout salad. I use the bounty of ingredients and my secret weapon, rotisserie chickens, to easily create everything from Deli-Style Chicken Salad of plump chicken shreds and mayonnaise to the refreshing Tropical Toss with fresh mango slices and pineapple chunks.

Do not limit yourself to the recipes in this chapter when you think chicken and salad. There are many dishes you can quickly put together without a recipe. These are just a few ideas to get you started:

- Grab a Caesar salad kit or two of romaine lettuce, croutons, and dressing in the produce section and arrange the lettuce on plates. Give a rotisserie chicken breast a quick chop, sprinkle it over the lettuce and croutons, drizzle on the dressing, and lunch is served. This carries well to work if you pack everything in separate containers and put it together at lunchtime.
- Quickly convert deli-case potato salad to a full meal by adding chunks of rotisserie chicken and green beans, shredded carrots, or other vegetables to taste.
- Cut a few rotisserie chickens into serving pieces and arrange on a platter with jarred antipasto vegetables, roasted pepper slivers, slices of mozzarella, and crusty bread slices for a quick party platter.

- Stir together about 2 cups of chopped rotisserie chicken, a 15-ounce can of rinsed and drained black beans, 1 cup of frozen corn kernels, half of a red bell pepper, chopped, and half of a green bell pepper, chopped. Add a little chopped red onion, stir in salsa, and you have a quick Tex-Mex salad.
- Stir chicken chunks into deli rice salad and add a handful of walnuts or raisins, if you are in the mood.
- Mound a ready-to-eat salad mix with arugula on a plate. Top with ripe pear slices and slivers of rotisserie chicken breast. Sprinkle Gorgonzola or other blue-veined cheese and walnuts over the top and drizzle with a bottled raspberry vinaigrette.
- For a quick tostada, pile lettuce on a ready-to-eat tostada shell. Top with chunks of rotisserie chicken, a handful of black beans and corn, and a sprinkling of already-shredded Mexican blend cheese. Spoon on salsa and sour cream, as desired.

Think rotisserie chicken and salad when you need a light dish to take along, when you are looking for a cool meal on a hot day, or when you need a quick meal on the run. Remember, it's as simple as 1-2-3! You will be happy you did.

CALIFORNIA COBB SALAD

—Makes 4 servings—

Ingenuity and hunger were at work in the kitchen late one night when Bob Cobb, the owner of the legendary Brown Derby restaurant in Los Angeles, is said to have created this now classic salad for a friend. I love to put this crisp, pretty, and colorful salad together when I want greens and am in search of a lot of distinct flavors in a salad. Remove any tough stems from the watercress and cut the avocado last so that it does not brown.

3 cups torn romaine lettuce leaves

1 cup watercress leaves (about 1 bunch)

1 cup torn curly endive leaves

1½–2 cups bite-size chunks rotisserie chicken breast, skin removed

1 large tomato, chopped (about 1 cup)

2 hard-cooked eggs, finely chopped (a generous ½ cup)

4 slices bacon, cooked crisp and crumbled

3 green onions, thinly sliced

1 large avocado, chopped

¼ cup crumbled blue cheese

Bottled balsamic salad dressing

Freshly ground black pepper

1. Toss the romaine, watercress, and endive leaves together on a large serving platter. Mound the chicken, tomato, eggs, bacon, onions, and avocado in strips over the greens. Sprinkle the blue cheese on top.

2. Drizzle lightly with about ⅔ cup of the dressing. Toss the salad and serve, passing extra dressing and ground pepper at the table.

▶ Note
- The peppery note of watercress and the pleasantly bitter flavor of endive are nice offsets to the richness of the bacon, eggs, and avocado in this salad.

Produce Pick: Look for avocados that give just a little when you press very lightly. To get the flesh out, slice the avocado in half lengthwise, stopping at the pit, and then lift off the top. Scoop out the pit with a spoon, then scoop out the flesh.

Lighter Touch: Use the egg whites instead of the whole egg if you are watching your cholesterol.

GREEK SALAD

—Makes 3-4 servings—

This salad is simply delicious and bursting with the full flavors, colors, and juiciness of the Mediterranean. The roasted chicken flavor and the richness of the olives are great complements to the lemony tang of the dressing. This is one of my favorites to put together for a quick light meal. Round out the meal with pita bread.

LEMON OREGANO DRESSING

3 tablespoons freshly-squeezed lemon juice

2 tablespoons red wine vinegar

2½ tablespoons olive oil

1 clove garlic, peeled and smashed

½ teaspoon dried oregano, crumbled between the fingers

¼ teaspoon salt

Pinch of pepper

SALAD

5 cups torn romaine lettuce leaves (about three-fourths of a 10-ounce package)

2 cups baby spinach leaves (about one-fourth of a 10-ounce package)

2 to 2½ cups bite-size chunks rotisserie chicken breast, skin removed

1 medium cucumber, peeled and cut into ¼-inch chunks

1 large tomato, chopped (about 1 cup)

1 cup pitted kalamata olives, drained (cut in half or quarters if large)

½ medium red onion, thinly sliced (about 1 cup)

½ cup crumbled feta cheese

1. **MAKE THE DRESSING:** Combine the dressing ingredients in a jar and shake well to combine. Set aside.

2. **MAKE THE SALAD:** Toss the salad ingredients together in a large bowl.

3. Remove the garlic clove from the dressing. Drizzle the salad to taste with the dressing, toss again, and serve.

▶ **Notes**

- Kalamata olives are Greek in origin. These purplish black olives are flavorful and tangy. Look for them in jars on the supermarket shelves or in the refrigerated deli cases.
- If you cannot find the olives pitted, you may find some kalamata olives that come with a little cut down the side. All you have to do is peel the olive away from the pit. Otherwise, put them on a cutting board, give them a quick whack with the side of a large knife, or press down on them with your hand, and lift the flesh away.

In a Pinch: Use your favorite bottled Greek vinaigrette if time is tight.

Lighter Touch: Use half the amount of olives called for and take a few minutes to cut them in half. You will get a lot of olivey richness with fewer calories.

Just You or Two: This is great for one or two. Adjust the salad ingredients to fit your appetite. You can cut the salad dressing in half or make a full batch and pop any extra in the fridge for a few days. You will have a homemade treat ready for another time.

Play It Again: You can refrigerate any *undressed* salad until the next day and then just toss it with a little dressing and tuck it inside a pita round for a tasty sandwich.

Company's Coming: This is great for summertime entertaining. For parties I like to arrange the chicken, cucumber, tomatoes, and olives on top of the greens. I scatter the onion slices over the top, sprinkle with the feta, and toss at the table with the dressing for a little quick drama.

MOROCCAN COUSCOUS, RAISIN, AND MINT SALAD

—Makes 6 servings—

Rotisserie chicken and couscous are a speedy match made in heaven. The chicken is ready to eat, and the couscous cooks in just a few minutes. Let this refreshing salad chill for about thirty minutes before serving so that the flavors have a chance to come together. Serve with pita bread or another favorite Middle Eastern flatbread.

COUSCOUS

1 cup dry, plain, quick-cooking couscous
1½ cups water
1 teaspoon salt

1 teaspoon olive oil
1 tablespoon ground cinnamon
2 teaspoons finely grated orange zest

DRESSING

1 (8-ounce) container plain yogurt (1 cup)
¾ cup orange juice
1 cup firmly packed mint leaves (about 1 bunch), stems removed

SALAD

1½ cups coarsely shredded rotisserie chicken, skin removed and meat pulled apart by hand
3 medium green onions, thinly sliced (about ½ cup)

½ cup raisins
½ cup already-shredded matchstick-size carrots
½ cup slivered almonds
¼ teaspoon salt

1. **MAKE THE COUSCOUS:** Prepare the couscous according to the package directions, using the water, salt, and oil. Add the cinnamon and orange zest as soon as the moisture is absorbed.

Fluff the couscous with a fork, scoop it into a medium bowl, and let cool until no steam rises when it is fluffed. While the couscous is cooling, make the dressing.

2. **MAKE THE DRESSING:** Combine the yogurt, orange juice, and mint leaves in a food processor or blender and process until the yogurt and orange juice are combined and the mint is finely chopped.

3. **MAKE THE SALAD:** Add the salad ingredients to the cooled couscous and toss well to combine. Do not stir the couscous, or the grains will stick together. Pour the dressing over the salad and toss to combine. Do not stir. Chill for 30 minutes before serving.

▶ Notes

- Orange zest is the colorful part of the orange peel. Avoid the bitter white part or pith underneath. To grate, cover a four-sided box grater with plastic wrap and pull the orange down the side of the grater. Or use one of the new microplane zester-graters available in cookware stores.
- For added flavor, toast the almonds. Place in a conventional or toaster oven at 350° F until fragrant and toasted, 5–7 minutes, stirring two or three times. Watch them carefully since they can go from nicely toasted to burned very quickly.

CHINESE CHICKEN SALAD

—Makes about 4 servings—

———— ⚬ ————

The appeal of this salad comes from the layers of enticing flavors in the dressing and the tasty mix of crispy salad ingredients. Use bottled dressing or make your own. Either way, you will have this salad ready faster than you can say, "Takeout."

1½ cups canned ready-to-eat chow mein noodles

SALAD

1 (8-ounce) package coleslaw mix (about 3½ cups, not packed)

2 cups large shreds rotisserie chicken, skin removed and meat pulled apart by hand

2 cups shredded iceberg lettuce

1 bunch green onions, diagonally sliced into 1-inch pieces

½ cup already-shredded matchstick-size carrots

Chinese chicken salad dressing, to taste, bottled or homemade

GARNISH

½ cup chopped peanuts (optional)

1. Preheat the oven to 350° F. Place the noodles on a baking sheet and toast until hot and crispy, 5–7 minutes, stirring occasionally. Set aside.

2. **MAKE THE SALAD:** Combine the salad ingredients and 1 cup noodles in a large bowl. Toss well to combine. Shake the dressing, pour over the salad, and toss again. Sprinkle the remaining ½ cup noodles and peanuts over the top, if using. Serve immediately.

Feeling Flush: If you have a few minutes to prepare your own dressing, combine these ingredients in a jar and shake well: $1/3$ cup rice vinegar, 3 tablespoons vegetable oil, 2 tablespoons honey, 1 tablespoon dark sesame oil, 1 tablespoon soy sauce, 1 tablespoon jarred chopped ginger, 2 teaspoons Dijon mustard, 1 teaspoon jarred minced garlic. You are in for a treat.

Just You or Two: Cut the recipe in half and dress only what you are going to eat.

Do-Ahead Tip: Shred the chicken and slice the onions ahead of time. Refrigerate separately.

REFRESHING LEMON GRAPE SALAD

—Makes 4 servings—

Refreshing and easy, this light salad takes full advantage of summer's fruit bounty. The yogurt dressing with a splash of fresh lemon juice adds a sweet tartness that brings the salad together. Perfect for a luncheon or a light dinner.

DRESSING

2 (6-ounce) containers lemon yogurt (about 1¼ cups)

2 tablespoons freshly-squeezed lemon juice

2 tablespoons finely chopped mint

Pinch of salt

SALAD

2 cups bite-size chunks rotisserie chicken, skin removed

1 cup bite-size chunks cantaloupe

½ cup red seedless grapes, cut in half lengthwise

½ cup green seedless grapes, cut in half lengthwise

⅓ cup finely chopped red bell pepper

⅓ cup slivered almonds, toasted

3 cups baby spinach leaves, on a serving platter

1. **MAKE THE DRESSING:** Stir the ingredients together in a large bowl.

2. **MAKE THE SALAD:** Combine the salad ingredients, except the spinach leaves, in the bowl with the dressing. Stir well to combine. Serve on top of the spinach leaves.

- To toast the almonds, place in a conventional or toaster oven at 350° F until fragrant and toasted, 5–7 minutes, stirring two or three times. Watch them carefully since they can go from nicely toasted to burned very quickly.

Lighter Touch: Already light, you can lighten this even more by choosing a 99% fat-free yogurt.

Company's Coming: A great pick for summertime entertaining.

SOUTHWESTERN TACO SALAD

—Makes 4 servings—

—— ✎ ——

This salad is as easy as easy can get. A great way to boost vegetable and legume intake, it is a favorite light meal. The combination of ranch dressing and salsa gives a cool bite. In cool weather, I like to serve this with a bowl of piping hot tomato soup.

DRESSING

¾ cup bottled light ranch salad dressing
½ cup salsa

SALAD

6 cups torn romaine lettuce leaves
2 cups bite-size chunks rotisserie chicken
1½ cups broken tortilla chips
1 (11-ounce) can Mexican-style corn with red and green bell peppers, drained (about 1⅓ cups)

1 cup drained black beans, rinsed if desired
1 small avocado, chopped
Already-shredded Cheddar cheese, to taste
½ teaspoon chili powder

1. **MAKE THE DRESSING:** Stir the ingredients together in a small bowl. Set aside.

2. **MAKE THE SALAD:** Combine the ingredients except the chili powder in a large bowl, using as much cheese as desired. Add the dressing and toss. Sprinkle with the chili powder and serve immediately.

THREE-BEAN PASTA SALAD

—Makes 6–8 servings—

Jarred three-bean salad was one of my favorite salads as a child. I still love the bite and the medley of beans. Now, I also appreciate the quick and easy way it pairs with other vegetables and pasta, and my trusty chicken, of course, to make a great full-meal salad. You can find the bean salad in cans on the shelf or in the refrigerated deli case.

SALAD

1 teaspoon salt

8 ounces dried bow-tie pasta, not mini (about 2 cups)

1 (15-ounce) can three-bean salad, drained and liquid reserved

2½ cups bite-size chunks rotisserie chicken

1 cup grape or cherry tomatoes, cut in half

1 cup finely chopped raw cauliflower

1 large rib celery, sliced on the diagonal into ¼-inch pieces

½ cup thinly sliced red onion

DRESSING

½ cup reserved liquid from the bean salad

3 tablespoons olive oil

2 tablespoons Dijon mustard

1 teaspoon dried dill weed, crumbled between the fingers

1 teaspoon jarred minced garlic

1 teaspoon freshly-squeezed lemon juice

Salt and pepper, to taste

1. **MAKE THE SALAD:** Cook the pasta according to the package directions until just tender to the bite using 1 teaspoon salt. Drain and then rinse under cold water. Shake any excess water off the pasta and place in a large salad bowl. Add the remaining salad ingredients and stir well to combine.

2. **MAKE THE DRESSING:** Place the dressing ingredients, except the salt and pepper, in a jar. Shake well to combine. Drizzle the dressing on the salad to your taste. Toss gently to mix in. You may not use all the dressing. Add salt and pepper and serve. Or chill before serving and add more dressing at serving time, if desired.

Company's Coming: Great potluck, buffet, or picnic fare.

Do-Ahead Tip: To make a day ahead, mix the salad and make the dressing ahead. Refrigerate separately and quickly combine at serving time.

RANCH RICE SALAD

—Makes 3-4 servings—

This is my refreshing rotisserie chicken version of a ham salad my mother made when I was growing up. I love the full flavor the chicken brings. Ranch dressing replaces her mayonnaise, and I brighten up the dressing a little with chopped roasted red peppers. The cool flavors make this colorful salad a real family pleaser, perfect for light spring and summer meals.

DRESSING

2/3 cup bottled ranch dressing
1/2 cup chopped roasted red peppers
3 tablespoons light sour cream

1 1/2 teaspoons dried dill weed, crumbled
  between the fingers
1/2 teaspoon salt

SALAD

3 cups firmly cooked and cooled long-grain
  rice, not instant
2 cups bite-size chunks rotisserie chicken, skin
  removed
1 cup mild Cheddar cheese cubes or already-
  shredded mild Cheddar cheese

1/2 cup frozen peas, thawed
2 medium green onions, thinly sliced
Pepper, to taste
6 cups torn romaine lettuce leaves or baby
  spinach leaves

1. **MAKE THE DRESSING:** Mix the dressing ingredients together in a medium bowl.

2. **MAKE THE SALAD:** Add all the salad ingredients except the pepper and the lettuce to the bowl with the dressing. Stir gently but thoroughly. Add pepper and stir. Serve on lettuce leaves.

▶ Notes

- Be sure not to overcook the rice. It must be firm, or you will have a mushy salad.
- Pick up ready-to-eat cheese cubes in the cheese section of the refrigerator case and save yourself some time.
- Be sure to use mild Cheddar cheese; the taste of sharp cheese is overpowering in this salad.

Lighter Touch: Use reduced-fat dressing to lighten this up.

Company's Coming: This is a great springtime or summer luncheon or shower dish.

MEDITERRANEAN CHICKEN SALAD NIÇOISE

—Makes 4 servings—

———— ✄ ————

Rotisserie chicken stands in nicely for the classic tuna in this pretty, delightful all-in-one version of the classic Salade Niçoise. Mom and I knew that this was a winner the first time I made it. Boil the potatoes gently to keep the skins on. Offer crusty rolls to round out the meal.

1 teaspoon salt
½ pound fresh green beans, ends trimmed
4 medium red potatoes (about 1 pound), scrubbed

DRESSING

⅓ cup olive oil
3 tablespoons red wine vinegar
2 teaspoons Dijon mustard

1 teaspoon jarred minced garlic
¼ teaspoon salt
⅛ teaspoon white pepper

SALAD

2 cups bite-size chunks rotisserie chicken, skin removed
10 cherry tomatoes, cut in quarters lengthwise
½ cup thinly sliced red onion semicircles

⅓ cup kalamata olives, pitted and coarsely chopped
Salt and pepper, to taste
6 cups torn romaine leaves

1. Put a large pot of water on to boil over medium-high heat and place a colander over a plate next to the stove. When the water reaches a boil, add the salt and green beans. Cook until the beans are just tender to the bite, 3–5 minutes depending on the size of the beans. Use a slotted spoon to remove the beans to the colander. Do not discard the water. Run cold water on the beans to stop the cooking, shaking off any excess water.

2. Return the water to a boil. Cut the unpeeled potatoes into ½-inch cubes (you should have about 3 cups) and place in the boiling water. Lower the heat so that the potatoes boil gently. Cook until just tender when pierced with a fork, about 12 minutes. While the potatoes are boiling, pat the beans dry, cut into 2-inch pieces, and place in a large bowl. (You should have about 2 cups.) Drain the potatoes and let cool.

3. **MAKE THE DRESSING:** While the potatoes are cooling, place the dressing ingredients in a jar, shake well to mix, and set aside.

4. **MAKE THE SALAD:** Add the chicken, tomatoes, onion, and olives to the bowl with the beans. Toss well to combine and then add the cooled potatoes and toss again. Drizzle the dressing over the top and toss. Season with salt and pepper. Divide the lettuce among 4 plates and spoon the salad on top.

In a Pinch: The lush bite of kalamata olives is essential to this salad. Do not substitute other olives.

Play It Again: This keeps well overnight.

Company's Coming: This is pretty and easy party fare. Remember it when you want to offer the goodness of vegetables in an easy but impressive salad.

Do-Ahead Tip: Refrigerate the ingredients separately overnight. Combine and toss with the dressing at serving time.

BUFFALO PASTA SALAD

—Makes 4–6 servings—

Not for tender tongues, this colorful and fiery salad is great paired with thick slices of bread and cold beer. The blend of chili sauce, pepper sauce, and cayenne lets the refreshing flavors come right through while still packing a punch. The heat sneaks up on you, so resist the urge to add more hot stuff to the bowl. Instead, let any asbestos-mouthed guests add it to their servings.

DRESSING

1 (8-ounce) bottle blue cheese dressing, regular or light (about 1 cup)

½ cup crumbled blue cheese

⅓ cup light sour cream

3 tablespoons bottled chili sauce

1–2 tablespoons liquid pepper sauce

2 teaspoons paprika

1 teaspoon salt

½ teaspoon cayenne

SALAD

8 ounces uncooked rotini, cooked firm according to package directions and rinsed in cold water (about 4 cups cooked)

2½ cups bite-size chunks rotisserie chicken, skin removed

2 large ribs celery, sliced into ¼-inch pieces

1 cup already-shredded matchstick-size carrots

1 large red bell pepper, chopped (about 1 cup)

1 bunch green onions, thinly sliced (about 1 cup)

2 tablespoons finely chopped flat-leaf (Italian) parsley

1 (10-ounce) bag torn romaine lettuce leaves (about 7 cups)

1. **MAKE THE DRESSING:** Stir the ingredients together in a small bowl. Set aside.

2. **MAKE THE SALAD:** Shake any excess water off the pasta and place in a large bowl. Add the remaining salad ingredients except the lettuce, and stir. Pour the dressing over the salad and stir well to combine. Line a platter with the lettuce and spoon the salad on top.

Lighter Touch: Reduced-fat salad dressing lightens this up.

Do-Ahead Tip: This is a company dish that men seem to love. You can whip this up after guests arrive, or you can prepare all the salad ingredients except the parsley a day in advance and refrigerate them separately in plastic bags. The next day simply chop the parsley, make the dressing, and stir everything together.

DELI-STYLE CHICKEN SALAD

—Makes 4 servings—

The lemon juice adds a nice tang, cutting a little of the richness in this homemade version of the chicken salad that is so popular in delis. An uncomplicated salad that relies on moist chicken and the sweet crunch of fresh celery, this is great as a sandwich or spooned onto crackers. Spoon into hollowed-out tomatoes for a pretty luncheon dish.

2 cups large shreds of rotisserie chicken, meat pulled apart by hand
½ cup mayonnaise
3 tablespoons thinly sliced green onions

1 teaspoon freshly-squeezed lemon juice
2 large ribs celery, sliced about ¼-inch thick (about 1 cup)
Salt and pepper, to taste

1. Combine the chicken, mayonnaise, onions, and lemon juice in a large bowl. Stir well with a rubber spatula, pressing against the side of the bowl to mash the chicken together a little. Stir in the celery. Season with salt and pepper.

VARIATION

Diner Chicken Melt:

Stir 2 tablespoons of drained pickle relish into ¾ cup of the chicken salad. Spread on a slice of bread and sprinkle with about ⅓ cup of already-shredded Cheddar cheese. Place in a toaster oven or under a preheated broiler until the cheese melts, about 2 minutes. Top with a thick tomato slice.

Lighter Touch: Use reduced-fat mayonnaise.

Produce Tip: To keep celery fresh longer, cut the root off and stand the ribs in a jar of water. Cover with a plastic bag and refrigerate.

TROPICAL TOSS

—Makes 4 servings—

Ready-to-eat mango slices that are available in the refrigerated section of the produce section are paired here with tender shreds of rotisserie chicken and tried-and-true pineapple and bananas for a lusciously quick passport to the tropics. You mix the zippy fruit juice dressing right in the bowl, making cleanup as easy as the salad itself.

½ cup sweetened flaked coconut (see Note)

DRESSING

1 (20-ounce) can pineapple chunks in juice, undrained

3 tablespoons frozen orange juice concentrate, thawed

2 tablespoons freshly-squeezed lime juice

1 tablespoon vegetable oil

1 teaspoon jarred chopped ginger, or 1 teaspoon freshly grated ginger and 1 teaspoon firmly packed light brown sugar

⅛ teaspoon red pepper flakes, crushed between the fingers

⅛ teaspoon salt

SALAD

3 cups large shreds rotisserie chicken, skin removed and meat pulled apart by hand

1½ cups firmly packed jarred, drained mango slices, cut into ½-inch chunks

1 medium banana, sliced into ¼-inch pieces

3 medium green onions, thinly sliced (about ½ cup)

½ cup finely chopped red bell pepper (about half of a large pepper)

4 cups torn romaine leaves

1. Spread the coconut on a baking sheet and toast in a 350°F oven, stirring frequently, for 5–7 minutes or until light gold.

2. **MAKE THE DRESSING:** Drain the pineapple chunks, reserving 3 tablespoons of the juice. Set the chunks aside for the salad. Whisk the 3 tablespoons of pineapple juice and the other dressing ingredients together in a large serving bowl.

3. **MAKE THE SALAD:** Add the pineapple chunks, chicken, mango, banana, green onions, and bell pepper to the bowl. Toss well to combine.

4. Divide the lettuce among 4 plates. Mound the salad in the center of the lettuce and sprinkle with the toasted coconut.

▶ Note

- Coconut burns quickly and is very easy to forget. I suggest that you whistle a tune and watch the coconut rather than trying to do anything else while you toast it.
- Rinse your hands after crushing the pepper flakes to prevent burning your eyes.

Lighter Touch: This salad is already light because it has just a touch of oil and the flavor comes from fruit. Go easy on the coconut to lighten it up a little more.

Do-Ahead Tips: Make the dressing up to a day ahead and refrigerate in a measuring cup. Shred the chicken, cut the mango, slice the green onions, and chop the red pepper in advance and refrigerate separately. At serving time, toast the coconut and pour the dressing into the bowl. Slice the banana, add the reserved salad ingredients, and toss. Spoon onto the lettuce and serve.

CHOPPED BARBECUE CHICKEN SALAD

—Makes 4 servings—

This is my version of one of my favorite lunches at a barbecue stop near my office some years ago. I find the combination of crisp, juicy lettuce, shredded carrots, and plump chopped chicken just as satisfying now as it was then. This is even faster if you pick up carrots, cucumbers, and eggs at the salad bar.

2 cups chopped rotisserie chicken

½ cup bottled barbecue sauce

4 cups prepackaged torn romaine lettuce leaves

2 cups coleslaw mix

1 cup already-shredded carrots

1 medium cucumber, peeled, cut into quarters lengthwise, and sliced crosswise into ¼-inch pieces (about 1½ cups)

2 hard-cooked eggs, chopped (about ½ cup)

2 medium tomatoes, chopped

½ bunch green onions, thinly sliced crosswise (about ½ cup)

4 radishes, chopped

Already-shredded sharp Cheddar cheese, to taste

Croutons

Bottled Italian or ranch dressing

1. Stir the chicken and barbecue sauce together in a large bowl. Toss with the remaining salad ingredients except the croutons and dressing, adding cheese as desired. Sprinkle with croutons. Toss and serve with the dressing on the side.

Lighter Touch: Choose reduced-fat cheese and use just the whites of the eggs.

Just You or Two: It is easy to make this for one or two. Simply use half of everything.

Play It Again: Wrap any leftovers in a burrito-size flour tortilla for a quick wrap sandwich. Drizzle on the dressing and roll into a cylinder.

OVERNIGHT PARTY SALAD

—Makes 8–10 servings—

I call this one of my rotisserie chicken bonuses. Overnight salads, with their layers of vegetables resting under mayonnaise dressings, were made popular in the 1950s. The concept is perfect for today's busy lives since they are delicious, vegetable rich, and you can put them together quickly. I like the dressing with a little more pizzazz. The flavors come together overnight, and your party is waiting for you the next day.

SALAD

6 cups prepackaged torn romaine lettuce leaves (more than three-fourths of a 10-ounce bag)

2 cups baby spinach leaves

1 (15-ounce) can kidney beans, rinsed and drained

2 ribs celery, sliced about ¼-inch thick

2½ cups bite-size chunks rotisserie chicken

15 cherry tomatoes, cut in half

2 cups already-shredded carrots

1 large cucumber, peeled and chopped

DRESSING

1 (8-ounce) container light sour cream (about 1 cup)

½ cup Thousand Island dressing

1 teaspoon freshly-squeezed lemon juice

Pepper, to taste

1. **MAKE THE SALAD:** Toss the lettuce and spinach together in a large clear bowl. Remove half of the mixture and set aside. Spread the other half on the bottom of the bowl. Top with the remaining salad ingredients in layers. Spread the reserved lettuce and spinach mixture over the top.

2. **MAKE THE DRESSING:** Mix the ingredients together in a small bowl. Spread on top of the salad. Cover the bowl with plastic wrap and refrigerate overnight. To serve, use a large serving spoon to scoop down through the salad.

Just You or Two: Use a smaller bowl and cut back on the quantities if you need fewer servings.

Do-Ahead Dish: You can also make this in the morning and serve it that evening.

Company's Coming: Great for entertaining. You can be a guest in your own home since dinner is ready.

PECAN WALDORF SALAD

—Makes 4 servings—

Richly toasted pecans and the anise-like favor of tarragon bring a refreshing twist to the classic Waldorf salad. I like to make this with Pippin apples, but you can use any firm, tart apples that your grocer has to offer.

DRESSING

⅓ cup mayonnaise
⅓ cup light sour cream
1 teaspoon freshly-squeezed lemon juice

1 teaspoon dried tarragon, crumbled between the fingers
¼ teaspoon salt, or to taste

SALAD

2½ cups bite-size chunks rotisserie chicken, skin removed
1 large rib celery, thinly sliced

¾ cup pecan pieces, toasted
2 medium tart apples
White pepper, to taste

1. **MAKE THE DRESSING:** Stir the dressing ingredients together in a large bowl.

2. **MAKE THE SALAD:** Add the chicken, celery, and pecans to the bowl with the dressing. Cut the unpeeled apples into ½-inch dice and add to the bowl. Stir gently to combine and season with pepper.

▶ Note

- To toast the nuts, place in a conventional or toaster over at 350° F until fragrant and toasted, 5–7 minutes, stirring two or three times. Watch them carefully since they can go from nicely toasted to burned very quickly.

In a Pinch: If you don't have pecans, walnuts will work fine. They are a little richer and have a little less bite.

Lighter Touch: You can use a reduced-fat mayonnaise. The salad will be sweeter, but it will still be delicious.

Just You or Two: This keeps well enough that you can save any leftovers for lunch or a snack the next day.

Play It Again: Leftovers are great tucked in a pita round the next day.

Company's Coming: You can easily double this recipe for company, using $1\frac{1}{2}$ teaspoons of tarragon. Mound it on a platter and surround with an array of crackers.

JASMINE RICE AND GINGER SALAD *great!*

—Makes 4 servings—

Jasmine rice adds a fragrant flavor to this Asian-style salad. You can assemble the salad the night before if you like, then add the dressing at serving time. Choose a Thai marinade with soy sauce and ginger if you cannot find a Mandarin marinade.

- 3 cups cooked jasmine rice, cold (about 1 cup *1½ c)* uncooked rice)
- 2 cups shredded rotisserie chicken, pulled apart by hand
- 1 bunch green onions, thinly sliced (about 1 cup)
- 1 (8-ounce) can sliced water chestnuts, drained
- 1 medium seedless cucumber, peeled and sliced into ¼-inch half-circles
- ½ cup already-shredded carrots
- 1 tablespoon jarred chopped ginger *grated*
- ½ cup bottled Mandarin marinade
- ½ cup roasted chopped peanuts or cashews (optional)

1. Gently stir the ingredients, except the nuts, together in a large bowl. Serve immediately, sprinkling the nuts over each serving, if desired.

▶ Note
  - It used to be considered exotic, but jasmine rice is now packaged by national rice companies and can be found in the rice aisle in supermarkets.

"ALL READY" RAMEN SALAD

—Makes about 6 servings—

—— ✂ ——

You cannot get any faster than this fun salad. The vegetables are already shredded, the noodles are already cooked, the dressing is already made, and the chicken is already-roasted, of course. Just quick-slice a few green onions, squeeze a little lemon juice, and this pleasing favorite is ready to eat.

1 (8-ounce) package coleslaw mix

2 packages (3-ounces each) ramen noodles, with 1 chicken seasoning packet reserved

2½–3 cups large shreds rotisserie chicken, meat pulled apart by hand

1 bunch green onions, thinly sliced (about 1 cup)

1 (11-ounce) can mandarin orange segments, drained

½ cup slivered almonds (optional)

½ cup bottled Chinese Chicken Salad dressing

2 tablespoons freshly-squeezed lemon juice

1. Place the coleslaw mix in a large salad bowl. Hold the ramen noodles over the bowl and break them into small pieces. Add the chicken, onions, mandarin oranges, and almonds, if using. Toss well to combine. Sprinkle with the reserved seasoning packet and toss again. Drizzle the salad dressing and lemon juice on top. Toss well to combine. Serve immediately.

▶ Note

- Freshly-squeezed lemon juice brightens up the bottled dressing.

> **Just You or Two:** You can easily cut this recipe in half.

Company's Coming: This is great party fare. It goes together so quickly that you can actually prepare it in minutes at party time. Line a platter with red and green cabbage leaves, and spoon the salad on top.

MUFFALETTA SALAD

—Makes 6–8 servings—

It's party time Big Easy style with this layered-salad version of the classic New Orleans sandwich. Reminiscent of an antipasto with touches of panzanella, an Italian bread salad, this is tasty and unusual enough to spark a conversation or two. This spunky salad takes a lot of chopping, but it is well worth it. You will be finished chopping before party time since you need to make this a day in advance to let the flavors come together properly.

OLIVE SALAD

¾ cup chopped green olives with pimento stuffing

½ cup chopped kalamata olives

½ cup chopped mixed fresh red and green bell peppers

½ cup finely chopped red onion

3 tablespoons olive oil

2 tablespoons finely minced flat-leaf (Italian) parsley

1 tablespoon jarred minced garlic

½ teaspoon pepper

¼ teaspoon salt

SALAD BASE

1½ cups thinly sliced rotisserie chicken breast strips, 2-inches long by ¼-inch wide by ⅛-inch thick

4 ounces salami, cut into strips about 2-inches long by ¼-inch wide by ⅛-inch thick (about 1 cup)

4 ounces already-sliced smoked ham, cut into strips 2-inches long by ¼-inch wide by ⅛-inch thick (about 1 cup)

4 ounces already-sliced provolone cheese, cut into strips 2-inches long by ¼-inch wide (about 1 cup)

1 (5 or 6-ounce) box garlic and herb croutons

1 (16-ounce) jar Italian mix antipasto vegetables, drained and coarsely chopped

3 cups torn romaine lettuce leaves

Bottled ranch salad dressing or creamy Italian dressing

1. **MAKE THE OLIVE SALAD:** Stir the ingredients together in a medium bowl and set aside.

2. **MAKE THE SALAD BASE:** Toss the chicken, salami, ham, and cheese together. Spread half of the croutons in the bottom of a large glass bowl. Top with the antipasto vegetables and then spread half of the meat and cheese mixture on top. Cover with the lettuce and spread the remaining meat and cheese mixture on top. Place the olive salad on the meat and spread to the edge of the bowl. Sprinkle the remaining croutons over the top, press down lightly, cover with foil, and refrigerate overnight.

3. **TO SERVE:** Remove from the refrigerator about 15 minutes before serving. To serve, use a large serving spoon to scoop to the bottom of the bowl, going through all the layers. Drizzle to taste with the salad dressing.

Play It Again: This keeps well for a second day.

WHICH CAME FIRST?

You don't have to worry about which came first, the chicken or the egg, with these recipes. The chicken and the egg are served together. Chicken is not just for dinner, and eggs are not just for breakfast. These dishes can be served any time of day.

Some cooks shy away from cooking eggs because they fear that eggs are temperamental. Here are a few simple hints to turning out nice, tender eggs:

- Make sure that the whites are broken up when you beat the eggs. A pinch of salt helps.
- Do not cook the eggs over high heat, or the whites will toughen.
- When making omelets, continue to lift the edges of the egg to allow any uncooked egg to flow underneath. Raw egg is not good news.

Round out the meals according to when you are serving the dish. If the Asparagus Omelet is for breakfast, you might want to serve fruit and toast alongside. If it is for dinner, roasted potatoes might go well. Be flexible and keep both the eggs and the rotisserie chickens within easy reach in the fridge.

ASPARAGUS OMELET

—Makes 1 serving—

You can have an elegant omelet in no time with a rotisserie chicken, a few eggs, and a box of asparagus spears. I use a good Swiss cheese, but if you can find it, fontina is also delicious.

EGGS

2 large eggs
1 tablespoon water
½ teaspoon dried dill, crumbled between the
    fingers

Pinch of salt and pepper
1 tablespoon butter

FILLING

1 medium shallot, finely chopped (about
    1 generous tablespoon)
⅓ cup shredded Swiss cheese

⅓ cup chopped rotisserie chicken
½ cup 2-inch pieces frozen asparagus spears,
    thawed

1. Lightly beat the eggs, water, dill, salt, and pepper together in a small bowl. Melt the butter in a nonstick 8-inch omelet pan or skillet over medium heat. When the butter begins to foam and sizzle, pour the eggs into the skillet and tilt the pan to coat the bottom. Sprinkle with the shallot. Use a spatula to gently push the eggs toward the center, letting the uncooked egg flow underneath.

2. When the top of the egg has set and you do not see any pools of uncooked egg, sprinkle the cheese on top, leaving a ½-inch border around the edge. Spoon the chicken and asparagus over half of the eggs, and then use the spatula to fold the other half over the top. Press down lightly with the back of the spatula and use it to carefully slide the omelet onto the serving plate.

VARIATION

Spinach Omelet

Substitute ½ cup cooked, drained baby spinach leaves for the asparagus.

Just You or Two: Perfect for dining alone at breakfast, lunch, or dinner.

COBB FRITTATA

—Makes 4–6 servings—

Frittatas offer all the goodness of omelets without the fuss of folding. Perfect for brunch or a supper with friends, this tasty frittata is bursting with the delicious flavors of a Cobb salad and is pretty to boot. It is wonderful served hot or at room temperature, and you can whip it up and have it on the table in no time flat. A simple green salad and orange slices make the meal complete.

SPICE BLEND

1 teaspoon paprika
¼ teaspoon salt
¼ teaspoon white pepper

FILLING

10 large eggs
3 tablespoons water
1 bunch green onions, thinly sliced (about 1 cup), divided
2 tablespoons unsalted butter
1 tablespoon olive oil

10 cherry tomatoes, cut in quarters lengthwise
1½ cups chopped rotisserie chicken breast, skin removed
6 slices bacon, cooked until crisp and crumbled
½ cup crumbled blue cheese

TOPPING

1 medium avocado
½ cup light sour cream

1. Position a rack in the center of the oven and preheat the oven to 375° F. Select a 12-inch nonstick ovenproof skillet and wrap the handle in foil.

2. **MAKE THE SPICE BLEND:** Stir the ingredients together in a large bowl.

3. **MAKE THE FILLING:** Add the eggs and water to the spice blend and whisk just well enough to break up the eggs. Do not create a lot of foam. Whisk in ¾ cup of the onions and set aside.

4. Place the butter and oil in the skillet over medium heat. When the butter melts, add the cherry tomatoes and cook, stirring frequently, just until they start to wilt, about 2 minutes. Sprinkle the chicken and bacon over the tomatoes and pour the egg mixture evenly over the filling. Turn the heat to low and cook for 2 minutes. Sprinkle the cheese over the top.

5. Cook, uncovered, until the eggs begin to set on the bottom, about 3 more minutes. Use spatula to push the cooked eggs toward the center of the skillet. Let the uncooked eggs flow to touch the bottom of the skillet. Put the skillet in the oven and bake until the center is just firm to the touch, about 12 minutes. A knife inserted in the center should come out clean.

6. **MAKE THE TOPPING:** While the frittata bakes, cut the avocado into chunks. Stir the avocado together with the sour cream and the remaining onions. To serve, slide the frittata onto a serving platter or serve directly from the skillet. Cut into wedges and serve with the topping.

▶ Note
- Avocados turn brown after they are cut. The sour cream helps slow the browning.

> **Serve It Up:** Never cut into a nonstick pan since you can easily damage the finish. Use a non-stick spatula instead to cut the frittata if you want to serve from the skillet.

In a Pinch: You can use 8 slices of ready-to-serve bacon straight from the package.

Play It Again: This keeps well, and I enjoy leftovers for breakfast with a hot cup of coffee.

FAJITA OMELET

—Makes 1 serving—

Wake up to a sizzle with a fajita filling wrapped in tender eggs. You can multiply this recipe to make as many omelets as you need, pouring a scant ¹⁄₂ cup of eggs into the pan for each omelet.

FILLING

¹⁄₃ cup mixed red and green bell pepper strips, ¼-inch thick

¼ cup thinly sliced onion

¹⁄₃ cup rotisserie chicken chunks

1 teaspoon bottled dry fajita seasoning mix

OMELET

2 large eggs

1 tablespoon water

Pinch of salt and pepper

1 teaspoon finely chopped cilantro

1 tablespoon butter

¹⁄₃ cup already-shredded sharp Cheddar cheese

TOPPINGS (OPTIONAL)

Prepared salsa and sour cream

1. **MAKE THE FILLING:** Lightly coat an 8-inch nonstick omelet pan or skillet with cooking spray. Heat the pan over medium heat. Cut the bell pepper strips in half crosswise and add to the skillet along with the onions. Cook until the onions just begin to soften, about 4 minutes, stirring frequently. Add the chicken, fajita seasoning, and 2 tablespoons water. Stir well, and cook, stirring frequently, until the moisture is absorbed, about 2 minutes. Scoop the filling into a bowl and wipe the pan dry.

2. **MAKE THE OMELET:** Lightly beat the eggs with the water, salt, and pepper. Stir in the cilantro. Return the pan to the stove over medium heat and add the butter. When the butter begins to foam and sizzle, pour the eggs into the skillet and tilt the pan to coat the bottom with the egg mixture. Use a spatula to gently push the eggs toward the center, letting the uncooked egg flow underneath.

3. When the top of the egg has set and you do not see any pools of uncooked egg, sprinkle the cheese over the top, leaving a ½-inch border around the edge. Spoon the fajita filling over half of the eggs and then use the spatula to fold the other half over the top. Press down lightly with the back of the spatula and use it to carefully slide the omelet onto the serving plate. Spoon salsa and sour cream over the top if desired.

Just You or Two: Perfect for dining alone at breakfast, lunch, or dinner.

BELL PEPPER AND ONION SCRAMBLE

—Makes 4–6 servings—

This satisfies my craving for a fajita omelet when the whole family is at the table. Make a few batches of this and serve with mango slices for an easy company brunch.

EGGS

8 large eggs
1 cup already-shredded mild Cheddar cheese
1 tablespoon finely chopped cilantro

⅛ teaspoon salt
⅛ teaspoon pepper

BASE

3 tablespoons vegetable oil, divided
1 cup mixed red and green bell pepper strips
1 cup thinly sliced onions

1 cup bite-size chunks rotisserie chicken breast
4 teaspoons dry fajita seasoning mix
2 teaspoons jarred minced garlic

Tortilla chips
Prepared salsa

1. **MAKE THE EGG MIXTURE:** Lightly beat the eggs in a medium bowl. Add the remaining ingredients, mix to combine, and set aside.

2. **MAKE THE BASE:** Heat 2 tablespoons oil in a 12-inch nonstick skillet over medium-high heat. Add the bell peppers and onions, and cook, stirring frequently, until they just begin to

soften, about 4 minutes. Lower the heat to medium and add the chicken, fajita seasoning, and garlic. Cook for 2 minutes, stirring frequently.

3. Add the remaining tablespoon of oil. Stir the egg mixture and pour it into the pan. Cook, stirring frequently, until the eggs are as firm as you like. Spoon onto a platter and tuck tortilla chips alongside. Pass the salsa.

Lighter Touch: Try reduced-fat cheese.

Just You or Two: Cut the recipe in half.

PARMESAN MONTE CRISTO

—Makes 2 sandwiches—

This skillet-grilled treat is a really tasty French toast sandwich. The ham is simply a flavor accent, so it should be almost paper-thin to let the rotisserie chicken shine through.

EGG MIXTURE

3 large eggs
¼ teaspoon salt
⅓ cup milk
2 tablespoons honey mustard
½ teaspoon paprika

¼ teaspoon ground nutmeg
Pinch of cayenne
½ cup grated Parmesan cheese (powdery consistency)

SANDWICH FILLING

2 tablespoons butter, divided
6 slices firm white sandwich-style bread
Thinly sliced skinless rotisserie chicken breast to cover 2 slices of bread

2 very thin slices ham
2 slices Swiss cheese (about 1 ounce each)
Honey mustard or raspberry preserves (optional)

1. Preheat the oven to 300° F.

2. **MAKE THE EGG MIXTURE:** Using a fork, lightly beat the eggs and salt together in a shallow pan. Add the milk, mustard, paprika, nutmeg, and cayenne, and beat to combine. Beat in the cheese.

3. **MAKE THE SANDWICHES:** Melt 1 tablespoon butter in a 12-inch nonstick skillet over medium heat. Quickly dip 3 bread slices in the egg mixture, turning once and shaking off any

excess. The bread should be coated but not saturated. Place in the skillet and cook until golden brown, 3–4 minutes. Flip the slices over. Cover 1 slice of bread with chicken slices and top with a slice of ham. Place a slice of cheese on another slice of bread. Continue cooking until the undersides of the bread are light brown, about 3 minutes.

4. Slip a spatula under the slice of bread with no topping and put the hot side of the bread on top of the cheese, pressing down slightly. Lift up the slices and put them on top of the ham. Press down slightly and cook for 1 minute, then turn and cook 1 minute more on the other side. Place on a cookie sheet and keep warm in the oven. Repeat with the remaining slices of bread, egg mixture, and filling, adding the additional tablespoon of butter to the pan before adding the bread. Cut both sandwiches in quarters on the diagonal. Serve with more mustard or preserves, if desired.

▶ Note

- Traditionally these sandwiches are assembled in three layers and then dipped in the egg mixture and fried. I am a stickler for not serving undercooked eggs, so I sauté the egg-dipped toast before assembling the sandwiches.

QUICHE CARBONARA

—Makes one 9-inch quiche—

I just love the rich creaminess of fettuccine alla carbonara. This quick recipe captures the same flavors of bacon, cream, and egg in a light, airy quiche. Bacon is key to the flavor, so select a good-quality bacon and have fun with different types, such as apple-smoked or the wonderful Italian pancetta. Take the crust out of the freezer, then start assembling the rest of the ingredients.

1 cup bite-size chunks rotisserie chicken
    breast, skin removed
1 (9-inch) frozen deep-dish piecrust, thawed
3 large eggs
¼ teaspoon salt
¼ teaspoon cayenne

1¼ cups half-and-half
8 slices bacon, cooked and crumbled
1¼ cups already-shredded Parmesan cheese
1 tablespoon finely chopped flat-leaf (Italian)
    parsley
1 teaspoon jarred minced garlic

1. Preheat the oven to 400° F and line a baking sheet with foil. Sprinkle the chicken on the bottom of the crust. Lightly whisk the eggs, salt, and cayenne together in a large bowl. Whisk in the half-and-half. Stir in the remaining ingredients and pour over the chicken. Place on the baking sheet and bake until the outside is set and the center puffs slightly and jiggles just a little when you shake it, about 35 minutes. Let rest for 5 minutes before serving.

▶ Note
   • Traditionally pastas alla carbonara are made with pancetta, the salt-cured Italian bacon that comes in rolls. To use, uncoil the sausage-like roll and chop into medium-size pieces. Cook over medium heat until crispy, stirring frequently. Drain on paper towels before adding to the mixture.

SPINACH SKILLET SOUFFLÉ

—Makes 4–6 servings—

Beaten egg whites put the puff in this easy-to-prepare skillet soufflé. I keep a worry-free kitchen, so I whisk away any fear of a fallen soufflé by baking it right in the skillet instead of a soufflé dish designed to help it rise. Fancy enough for company but easy enough for the family, this is a terrific way to get protein, calcium, and veggies into reluctant children.

SPICE BLEND

3 tablespoons all-purpose flour
1 teaspoon paprika
½ teaspoon ground nutmeg

½ teaspoon dry mustard
½ teaspoon salt
¼ teaspoon cayenne, or to taste

SOUFFLÉ

1½ cups milk
1 cup fat-free less-sodium chicken broth
3 tablespoons unsalted butter
1 small onion, chopped (about ½ cup)
3 large eggs, separated
2 cups finely chopped rotisserie chicken, skin removed

1 (10-ounce) package frozen chopped spinach, thawed and squeezed dry
1 (8-ounce) package finely shredded sharp Cheddar cheese (2 cups)
2 additional large egg whites
½ cup already-shredded Parmesan cheese

1. **MAKE THE SPICE BLEND:** Stir the ingredients together in a small bowl and set aside.

2. **MAKE THE SOUFFLÉ:** Position a rack in the bottom third of the oven. Preheat the oven to 350° F. Combine the milk and broth in a 1-quart measuring cup and microwave until hot. Set aside.

3. Melt the butter in a 12-inch nonstick skillet over medium heat. Add the onion and cook, stirring frequently, until tender, about 3 minutes. Stir in the spice blend and cook for 2 minutes, stirring constantly. Do not brown. While continuing to stir, slowly add the hot milk mixture, forming a smooth paste before adding more liquid. Bring to a boil, still stirring constantly and being careful to stir into the corners of the pan. The mixture should be smooth and thick enough to coat the back of a spoon. Remove from the heat.

4. Beat the egg yolks lightly in a large bowl. Ladle the hot mixture into the egg yolks, ½ cup at a time, stirring constantly. Stir in the chicken, spinach, and Cheddar cheese. Set aside to cool. Rinse and dry the skillet, and then lightly coat it with nonstick cooking spray.

5. Meanwhile, with clean beaters, beat the 5 egg whites in a medium bowl until soft peaks form. Gently stir one-quarter of the beaten whites into the yolk mixture. Scoop the rest of the whites onto the top of the mixture and then gently stir them in. Gently pour the mixture into the skillet and sprinkle with the Parmesan cheese. Wrap the handle in foil if it is not ovenproof. Bake until the soufflé is set and the top is puffy and golden brown, about 30 minutes. Serve immediately, scooping out of the pan with 2 nonstick spoons. Do not cut into the pan with a knife or you will damage the nonstick surface.

▶ All About Eggs

Separating and beating eggs does not have to be tricky. Here are a few practical tips.

- *Separating eggs:* It is easier to separate the whites from the yolks when the eggs are just out of the refrigerator. The fat in yolks will stop the whites from beating, so I use three bowls when separating them. After cracking the egg, I pour the white into the other half of the shell. I pour the white into a cup and the yolk into a large bowl. If the white is free of specks of yolk, I pour it into a medium glass or stainless steel bowl that will hold all the whites. If it has yolk in it, I discard the white, wash out the cup, and try again.

- *Beating egg whites:* The beater and bowl must be free of fat for the whites to beat. Glass and stainless steel bowls work best (plastic holds fats, and aluminum can react with the whites). I wipe the bowl and beater with a touch of white vinegar before starting to help remove all traces of fat. Beat on low speed until foam begins to form and then increase the speed as the egg whites start to thicken. You will know that you have soft peaks when you lift the beaters straight out of the bowl and the egg whites on the tip fall over a little. The whites in the bowl should look smooth and be clump-free.

Company's Coming: Pretty, delicious, and elegantly easy, this is a great dish for brunch or dinner entertaining. Serve it with sliced tomatoes and your favorite white wine.

Play It Again: If you are lucky enough to have any leftovers, this reheats well in a microwave.

Lighter Touch: 1% milk works just fine.

SOUPS IN A SNAP

Homemade soups stir up memories. Unfortunately, a shortage of time has created a shortage of homemade soups since many people believe that you must chop forever and simmer the soup for hours to get a great soup to the table. This is not necessarily so, as you will discover with these recipes.

Rotisserie chickens are a wonderful springboard for creating a fast homemade soup. I pair my ever-trusty rotisserie chicken with the readily available sauces, rice mixes, canned beans, and ready-to-cook produce that line our shelves today and literally take a trip around the globe with chicken soup. These recipes use flavors from everywhere, from Thailand to Main Street America, with the Hot and Sour Soup and the Quick Chicken Chowder. There is something for everyone and for every occasion in this chapter. A great meal-in-one, the Wild Rice and Leek Soup would make a wonderful start to a formal dinner, while you cannot beat the Chunky Chicken Minestrone for a family dinner on a cool evening.

You will love making and serving these soups. And since they are so easy, you will be able to enjoy them anytime you please. So break out the soup bowls or tureen and enjoy!

HOMEMADE CHICKEN NOODLE SOUP

—Makes 4 servings—

Homemade chicken soup is truly comfort in a bowl. Few people have time these days to make soup, but with canned broth, baby carrots, and a rotisserie chicken, you can have a heartwarming homemade chicken soup on the table in a matter of minutes. The squirt of freshly-squeezed lemon juice brightens the flavor. Serve with crackers.

- 3 (14½-ounce) cans fat-free less-sodium chicken broth (about 5¼ cups)
- ½ cup water
- 1 tablespoon freshly-squeezed lemon juice
- 3 sprigs plus ¼ cup minced flat-leaf (Italian) parsley
- 1 bay leaf
- 1 large clove garlic, peeled and smashed
- 1 cup baby carrots
- 1½ cups uncooked vermicelli or angel-hair pasta *noodles*
- ⅓ cup finely chopped celery (optional)
- 2 cups bite-size chunks rotisserie chicken, skin removed and meat pulled apart by hand
- Salt and pepper, to taste

1. Combine the chicken broth, water, lemon juice, parsley sprigs, bay leaf, and garlic in a medium saucepan with a lid. Stir, cover the pan, place over high heat, and bring to a boil. Meanwhile, slice the carrots crosswise into ½-inch rounds.

2. When the mixture reaches a boil, lower the heat to medium and stir in the sliced carrots, vermicelli, and celery if using. Cover the pan, leaving the top slightly ajar, and cook, stirring occasionally, until the noodles are almost tender, about 5 minutes.

3. Stir in the chicken. Cover and simmer until the noodles are tender and the carrots are slightly soft, 3–5 minutes. Season with salt and pepper. Use a slotted spoon to remove the parsley sprigs, bay leaf, and garlic. Ladle the soup into bowls and sprinkle with the minced parsley.

VARIATION

Homemade Chicken and Rice Soup:

Substitute 1 cup leftover cooked rice for the vermicelli. Add the rice to the hot broth mixture when you add the chicken. Or stir ½ cup uncooked long-grain white rice into the boiling chicken broth mixture and cook for 5 minutes before lowering the heat to medium and adding the carrots and optional celery. Proceed with the recipe, adding the chicken when the rice is almost tender, about 5 minutes after the carrots are added.

DOUBLE CORN AND CHICKEN CHOWDER

—Makes 4 servings—

This hearty chowder is full-flavored with pleasing bits of corn and a time-saving rustic touch from the red skins on the potatoes. The blend of spices in the Old Bay Seasoning instantly adds a nice complexity of flavor. Two teaspoons of the seasoning are quite mild; three give the chowder a little kick.

SPICE BLEND

3 tablespoons all-purpose flour
2–3 teaspoons Old Bay Seasoning

CHOWDER

6 slices bacon
1 large red bell pepper, chopped (about 1 cup)
1 large onion, chopped (about 1 cup)
2 large unpeeled red potatoes, cut into ¼-inch cubes (about ½ pound or 1½ cups), covered with cold water

2 (14½-ounce cans) fat-free less-sodium chicken broth (about 3½ cups)
2 cups large chunks rotisserie chicken, skin removed and meat pulled apart by hand
2 (14¾-ounce) cans cream-style corn
1½ cups corn kernels (fresh or frozen)
⅔ cup milk

1. **PREPARE THE SPICE BLEND:** Stir the ingredients together in a small bowl and set aside.

2. **MAKE THE CHOWDER:** Cook the bacon in a Dutch oven over medium heat until crispy, turning frequently. Put the bacon on a paper towel–lined plate, leaving the drippings in the pan. Add the bell pepper and onion to the pan and cook, stirring frequently, until the vegetables soften, about 5 minutes.

3. Drain the potatoes and add to the pan. Sprinkle the spice blend over all, and cook, stirring constantly, until the spices are fragrant, about 2 minutes. Add the chicken broth, raise the heat to medium high, and bring to a boil, stirring frequently. Lower the heat to medium and cook, covered, until the potatoes just begin to soften and the mixture has thickened slightly, about 7 minutes, stirring frequently.

4. Meanwhile, crumble the bacon and set aside. Stir in the chicken, corn, and milk. Return to a boil, stirring frequently to prevent sticking. Turn the heat to low and simmer, uncovered, until the potatoes are tender and the chowder has a thick, creamy consistency, about 15 minutes, stirring frequently. Ladle the soup into bowls. Sprinkle each serving with bacon.

▶ **Notes**

- Try a smoky bacon to add a special touch.
- I like to sprinkle the bacon on top to keep it crunchy but you can stir it in at the last minute, if you prefer.

Serve It Up: With a loaf of crusty bread, you have the perfect cozy meal for a brisk fall evening or damp winter afternoon.

CHINESE-STYLE NOODLE SOUP

—Makes 4–6 servings—

Just thinking about a bowl of this soothing soup makes me feel great. The broth is an important part of the soup, so don't skimp on the simmering time or the ingredients. The combination of noodles, vegetables, and chicken makes this a real meal-in-a-bowl.

BROTH

1 rotisserie chicken carcass

4 (14½-ounce) cans fat-free less-sodium chicken broth (about 7 cups)

5 (¼-inch thick) round slices of ginger, smashed

1 large carrot, cut into quarters, or ½ cup already-shredded carrots

½ large onion, unpeeled and cut in half

2 cloves garlic, smashed

½ stick cinnamon

5 peppercorns

2 teaspoons dark sesame oil

1 tablespoon freshly-squeezed lemon juice

NOODLES

4 ounces dry bean thread noodles

SOUP

1 (12 to 16-ounce) package frozen stir-fry vegetables

2 cups large shreds rotisserie chicken, pulled apart by hand

2 tablespoons matchstick-size pieces of peeled ginger

½ bunch green onions, thinly sliced (about ½ cup)

1. **MAKE THE BROTH:** Combine the ingredients except the sesame oil and lemon juice in a soup pot and bring to a boil over medium heat. Turn the heat to low and simmer uncovered for 30 minutes.

2. **PREPARE THE NOODLES:** Meanwhile, cover the noodles with very hot water and let rest for 15 minutes. The noodles will soften but should not be mushy. Drain and divide among 4 to 6 soup bowls.

3. Remove the pot from the heat after the broth has simmered for 30 minutes. Scoop the solids from the pot and discard. Stir in the sesame oil and lemon juice. Return the pot to the heat and bring the broth to a simmer.

4. **MAKE THE SOUP:** Stir the vegetables, chicken, and ginger into the soup pot. Cook just long enough to heat through. Remove from the heat. Ladle the soup over the noodles. Sprinkle with the onions and serve.

▶ Note
- Bean thread noodles, also known as mung bean threads, glass noodles, cellophane noodles, and Chinese vermicelli are clear, dry noodles made from the starches of green mung beans. You can find them in the Asian food aisle of many supermarkets or in Asian food markets.

In a Pinch
- If you do not have a cinnamon stick, stir in a pinch of ground cinnamon with the sesame oil and lemon juice.
- You can easily substitute one (3-ounce) package of ramen noodles for the cellophane noodles, keeping the seasoning packet for another use. Just break the noodles up and stir them into the pot along with the sesame oil and lemon juice. Simmer for 3 minutes, stirring occasionally. Then add the remaining ingredients.

CHICKEN AND LIME TORTILLA SOUP

great

—Makes 4 servings—

—✦—

I stir up this vegetable-rich version of the well-known Mexican chicken and tortilla soup when a zesty south-of-the-border soup is the order of the day. My chopping is kept to a minimum while the flavor is pumped up by taking advantage of what I call the "mix-in" vegetables that are so readily available: corn with red and green peppers added and diced tomatoes with peppers.

SOUP

2 tablespoons vegetable oil

1 small red onion, chopped (about 1 cup)

15 baby carrots, cut crosswise into thirds (about ¾ cup)

2 teaspoons bottled minced garlic *2-3 cloves*

1 teaspoon cumin seed

1 medium zucchini, cut into ¼-inch pieces (about 1 cup)

1 teaspoon chili powder

3 (14½-ounce) cans fat-free less-sodium chicken broth (about 5¼ cups) *~ 1 box*
+ ½ c water

1 (14½-ounce) can Mexican-style diced tomatoes with peppers

1 (11-ounce) can Mexican-style corn with red and green peppers, drained *frozen corn, 1 cup*

2 tablespoons canned mild diced chiles *1 fresh jalapeno*

½ teaspoon salt

2 cups large chunks rotisserie chicken, skin removed and meat pulled apart by hand

1 cup orzo

SERVING

1 large avocado

¼ cup chopped cilantro

3 tablespoons freshly-squeezed lime juice *~ 3 limes*

1 cup broken tortilla chips

1. **MAKE THE SOUP:** Heat the oil over medium heat in a large soup pot or 5–6-quart Dutch oven. Add the onion, carrots, garlic, and cumin seed. Stir well and cook, until the onion is ten-

+ jalapeno

der, about 5 minutes, stirring frequently. Add the zucchini and chili powder and cook, stirring frequently, just until the zucchini begins to soften, about 3 minutes.

orzo

2. Add the broth, tomatoes, corn, chiles, and salt. Stir well and bring to a boil. Cover, turn the heat to low, and simmer for 10 minutes, stirring occasionally. Add the chicken, stir well, and simmer about 3 minutes to heat the chicken.

3. While the soup is simmering, peel the avocado and cut it into chunks. Remove the soup from the heat and stir in the cilantro and lime juice. Spoon into warm soup bowls and top with the avocado chunks and tortilla chips.

VARIATION

For a spicier touch, stir 1–2 tablespoons finely chopped canned chipotle peppers in adobo sauce in along with the broth.

Lighter Touch: Make your own tortilla strips to reduce the fat. Preheat the oven to 350° F. Omit the chili powder from the soup. Cut 4 (6-inch) corn tortillas in half, then cut them into ½-inch strips. Put in a bowl, lightly coat with nonstick cooking spray, and toss with 1 teaspoon chili powder. Spread on a baking sheet and bake until crispy, 8–10 minutes.

Company's Coming: Pull out a big pot and double this for great casual get-together fare. Squeeze in about 5 tablespoons of lime juice. Toss the avocado chunks in a little lime juice to keep them nicely green.

QUICK CHICKEN CHOWDER

—Makes 3-4 servings—

When time is short, reach into your rotisserie chicken pantry and put together this hearty chowder. The frozen pepper strips and green onions keep chopping to a minimum, and the ready-to-use soup and vegetables make it all come together lickety-split. Serve with rolls to round out the meal. Our sons gave this true family pleaser a big thumbs-up. Be prepared to make this again and again.

SPICE BLEND

2 teaspoons paprika
1 teaspoon dried thyme, crumbled between the fingers

SOUP

1 tablespoon vegetable oil
1 cup frozen bell pepper strips, cut crosswise
    into ¼-inch dice
1 large bunch green onions, sliced
    (about 1 cup)
1 teaspoon jarred minced garlic
2 (10¾-ounce) cans condensed cream of
    potato soup, undiluted

1 (14½-ounce) can fat-free less-sodium
    chicken broth (about 1¾ cups)
1½ cups frozen mixed vegetables
1 large bay leaf
2 cups bite-size chunks rotisserie chicken, skin
    removed
Pepper, to taste

1. **MAKE THE SPICE BLEND:** Stir the ingredients together in a small bowl and set aside.

2. **MAKE THE SOUP:** Lightly coat a large soup pot or Dutch oven with nonstick cooking spray. Heat the oil in the pan over medium-high heat. Add the bell peppers and cook, stirring

constantly, until the moisture evaporates, about 3 minutes. Add the onions, garlic, and spice blend, and cook for 30 seconds, stirring constantly. Add the cream of potato soup, broth, mixed vegetables, and bay leaf, and stir well to blend. Bring to a boil, stirring constantly.

3. Add the chicken and stir well. Turn the heat to low and simmer, covered, for 10 minutes, stirring frequently to prevent sticking. The flavors will blend and the vegetables should be tender. Add the pepper, remove the bay leaf, and serve.

▶ Notes

- The cream of potato soup adds nice potato pieces without having to pick up a knife.
- If you use fresh bell pepper, cook in oil, stirring constantly until they just begin to soften, about 5 minutes.

Just You or Two: This is great when reheated the next day.

Do-Ahead Tip: You can make this a day in advance if you like. Do not freeze it.

ALPHABET SOUP

This lightning-quick pass-around recipe has been one of my favorites since a friend gave it to me years ago. These days I reach for a rotisserie chicken and have my version on the table whenever the kids ask for it. Serve with warm rolls and settle in for the alphabet game.

3 (14½-ounce) cans fat-free less-sodium chicken broth (about 5¼ cups)

2½ cups bite-size chunks rotisserie chicken

2 cups frozen mixed vegetables

1 (14½-ounce) can Italian-style diced tomatoes, undrained

½ cup water

2 bay leaves

1 cup dried alphabet pasta

3 green onions, thinly sliced (about ½ cup)

Salt and pepper, to taste

1. Bring the broth, chicken, vegetables, tomatoes, water, and bay leaves to a boil in a large saucepan or Dutch oven over medium-high heat. Turn the heat to low, stir in the pasta, and simmer, covered, until the pasta is tender, about 12 minutes. Remove from the heat and discard the bay leaves. Stir in the onions and add salt and pepper.

▶ Note
  • Italian-style diced tomatoes, seasoned with basil, garlic, and oregano save a measuring step.

CHUNKY CHICKEN MINESTRONE

—Makes 6–8 servings—

1½ hrs

Plump chunks of rotisserie chicken, ready-to-eat coleslaw mix, and a medley of canned beans make this thick, vegetable-rich offering a quick and hearty meal-in-a bowl. Brimming with flavors and textures, the steaming hot soup ladled on top of homemade Parmesan toasts gives a different twist to an already satisfying soup. Don't be put off by the long list of ingredients. This is really a pour-and-stir soup with very little chopping or tending needed. Add a tad more broth if you prefer a thinner soup.

VEGETABLES

3 tablespoons olive oil

1 large onion, chopped (about 1 cup)

1 cup baby carrots, cut crosswise into ¼-inch rounds

1 medium zucchini, cut into ¼-inch pieces (about 1 cup)

1 tablespoon jarred minced garlic

2 teaspoons dried Italian herb seasoning, crumbled between the fingers

SOUP

2 (14½-ounce) cans Italian stewed tomatoes (seasoned with garlic, oregano, and basil)

2 (14½-ounce) cans fat-free less-sodium chicken broth (about 3½ cups)

3 cups coleslaw mix with carrots

1 cup uncooked small bow-tie pasta or small elbow macaroni

2 tablespoons tomato paste

1 large bay leaf

2½ cups large chunks rotisserie chicken, pulled apart by hand

1 (15½-ounce) can garbanzo beans, undrained

1 (8¾-ounce) can red kidney beans, undrained

1 teaspoon salt

Black pepper, to taste ¼ (scant)

Parmesan toasts (recipe follows)

Already-shredded Parmesan cheese (optional)

1. **PREPARE THE VEGETABLES:** Heat the oil in a Dutch oven or large soup pot with a lid over medium-high heat. Add the onion and cook, stirring frequently, until it turns limp, about 3 minutes. Add the carrots to the pan and cook for 2 minutes, stirring frequently. Add the zucchini, garlic, and Italian seasoning. Cook, stirring constantly, until the zucchini just begins to soften, about 3 minutes.

2. **MAKE THE SOUP:** Add the stewed tomatoes, broth, coleslaw mix, pasta, tomato paste, and bay leaf. Break the tomatoes into pieces as you add them. Stir well, bring to a boil, and cook, covered, stirring frequently, until the pasta is very slightly soft to the bite, about 4 minutes. Turn the heat to medium-low so that the mixture simmers. Add the chicken, beans, salt, and pepper. Stir well and simmer, covered, until the beans and chicken are heated through and the flavors have blended, about 8 minutes. Stir frequently, and do not overcook the pasta. Make the Parmesan toasts while the soup is simmering.

3. To serve, place 2 Parmesan toasts on the bottom of each bowl. Remove the bay leaf and ladle the hot soup on top of the toasts. Sprinkle each serving with a little Parmesan cheese if desired.

PARMESAN TOASTS

16 ready-to-eat individual garlic crostini or garlic toasts (in bakery or deli section)
Olive oil
About ½ cup already-shredded Parmesan cheese

1. Preheat the broiler. Place the garlic crostini on a baking sheet so that they are close enough to touch. Lightly brush the toasts with oil and sprinkle with cheese. Broil just until the cheese melts and is bubbly, about 2 minutes.

- Open all the cans at once to make this go even faster.
- The beans, tomatoes, coleslaw, and roasted chicken make this soup pack a nutritional wallop.

In a Pinch: Instead of the Parmesan toasts, put about ¼ cup garlic croutons in the bottom of each soup bowl and sprinkle with 2 tablespoons already-shredded Parmesan cheese. Ladle the hot soup on top.

Do-Ahead Tip: You can make this a day ahead. Just cook the pasta separately, store it in a plastic bag in the refrigerator, and add it to the soup at serving time.

Just You or Two: You can easily cut this recipe in half. Watch the simmering time so you don't overcook the pasta.

HOT AND SOUR SOUP

—Makes 4 main-course servings—

What a delight to have a steaming hot homemade soup with all the good flavors of a Thai restaurant! This is great for lunch or a light dinner. I leave the seeds and the membranes in the chiles to give the soup a truly hot flavor. Be sure not to touch your eyes when handling the chiles, and wash your hands and the cutting surfaces right away to prevent burning yourself. The long list of ingredients adds flavor, not effort, to this simple-to-prepare soup.

BROTH

3 (14½-ounce) cans fat-free less-sodium chicken broth (about 5¼ cups)

1 cup water

3 serrano chiles, sliced crosswise into ⅛-inch pieces

2 teaspoons jarred minced garlic

1 teaspoon *each* finely grated lemon peel and lime peel

1 teaspoon *each* freshly-squeezed lemon juice and lime juice

1 (¼-inch) slice fresh ginger, unpeeled

FLAVOR BLEND

3 tablespoons distilled white vinegar

1 tablespoon dry sherry

2 teaspoons lite soy sauce

SOUP

1½ cups rotisserie chicken slivers, skin removed and meat preferably cut from breast

1½ cups thinly sliced Napa cabbage (about ⅛-inch across)

¾ cup small cubes medium-firm tofu

2 tablespoons cornstarch mixed with 2 tablespoons cold water

3 Roma tomatoes, chopped (about 1 cup)

3 green onions, thinly sliced (about ½ cup)

3 tablespoons coarsely chopped cilantro

1. **MAKE THE BROTH:** Combine the ingredients in a soup pot or Dutch oven. Stir well and bring to a boil over medium-high heat. Turn the heat to low and simmer, covered, for 20 minutes. Leave the pot on the stove and scoop out the solids with a slotted spoon. Discard. Bring the broth to a simmer again.

2. **MAKE THE FLAVOR BLEND:** Meanwhile, stir the ingredients together in a small bowl and set aside.

3. **FINISH THE SOUP:** Stir the chicken, cabbage, and tofu into the simmering broth. Stir the cornstarch mixture, then stir it into the pot and simmer, uncovered, for 3 minutes, stirring occasionally to heat the ingredients through and thicken the soup slightly. Remove from the heat and stir in the flavor blend, tomatoes, onion, and cilantro. Immediately ladle into serving bowls.

▶ Notes

- Cut the chicken along the grain to keep it from falling apart.
- To slice the cabbage, stack 2 to 3 leaves on top of one another, roll them up like a tube, and then slice crosswise into slivers.

In a Pinch: If you cannot find Napa cabbage, you can substitute green cabbage. Add it to the hot broth 2–3 minutes before the chicken and tofu.

Lighter Touch: This is light just as it is.

Company's Coming: If the rest of the meal is Thai takeout served in nice dishes, offer this as a first course to start the meal with a homemade touch.

CHEDDAR, BROCCOLI, AND CAULIFLOWER SOUP

—Makes 4–6 servings—

Flecks of bright green broccoli garnish the bowl in this creamy, calcium-rich soup. This rescue recipe is truly a lifesaver that you will reach into the cupboard to make again and again. It takes just a few minutes to put it together.

SPICE BLEND

2 teaspoons paprika
½ teaspoon ground nutmeg

½ teaspoon white pepper
¼ teaspoon salt, or to taste

SOUP

3 tablespoons butter
1 large onion, chopped (about 1 cup)
3 cups fresh broccoli florets, coarsely chopped
2 cups fresh cauliflower, coarsely chopped
2 (14½-ounce) cans fat-free less-sodium chicken broth (about 3½ cups)
1 (10¾-ounce) can condensed cream of potato soup, undiluted

2 cups bite-size chunks rotisserie chicken
1–1½ cups already-shredded sharp Cheddar cheese
⅓ cup already-shredded Parmesan cheese
1 (4-ounce) jar diced pimientos (½ cup)

1. **MAKE THE SPICE BLEND:** Stir the ingredients together in a small bowl and set aside.

2. **MAKE THE SOUP:** Melt the butter in a Dutch oven or soup pot over medium heat. Add the onion and cook, stirring frequently, until it softens, about 4 minutes. Sprinkle the spice blend over all and cook for 2 minutes, stirring constantly. Add the broccoli and cauliflower, and cook just until the broccoli begins to soften, about 4 minutes, stirring constantly. Do not brown. Add the broth, cream of potato soup, and chicken, and bring to a boil, stirring frequently.

3. Turn the heat to low and simmer, stirring frequently, until the cauliflower softens, about 8 minutes. Remove from the heat. Add the cheeses and pimientos, and stir well to combine the ingredients and melt the cheese. Ladle into soup bowls and serve immediately.

▶ Note

- Speed things along even more by picking up raw broccoli and cauliflower florets at the salad bar. Or look for bagged, ready-to-cook broccoli and cauliflower florets in the produce section.

EXTRA-QUICK BROCCOLI, CHEDDAR, AND BROWN RICE SOUP

—Makes 4 servings—

Variations on broccoli and Cheddar soup are very popular in restaurants. Many of the soups undoubtedly arrive from large companies already prepared. I reach for handy cans of cream of broccoli soup to give me a quick start at getting this homemade soothing soup on the table. The chicken and rice make it a complete meal. Serve with crusty rolls.

SPICE BLEND

1½ teaspoons paprika
½ teaspoon pepper
¼ teaspoon ground nutmeg

SOUP

2 tablespoons butter
1 small red onion, chopped (about ⅔ cup)
¾ cup instant brown rice
1 teaspoon jarred minced garlic
3½ cups milk
2 (10¾-ounce) cans condensed cream of broccoli soup, undiluted

2½ cups bite-size chunks rotisserie chicken, skin removed
¾ cup already-shredded sharp Cheddar cheese
3 tablespoons jarred diced pimientos
1 tablespoon Dijon-style mustard

1. **MAKE THE SPICE BLEND:** Stir the ingredients together in a small bowl and set aside.

2. **MAKE THE SOUP:** Melt the butter in a Dutch oven over medium heat. Add the onion and cook, stirring frequently, until soft, about 3 minutes. Add the rice, garlic, and spice blend, and

cook for 1 minute, stirring constantly. Add the milk and bring to a boil, stirring frequently, to prevent the milk from scorching. Lower the heat to keep the mixture at a simmer and cook, covered, for 5 minutes, stirring frequently. Turn the heat to low and stir in the soup and chicken. Simmer, covered, until heated through and the flavors blend, 8–10 minutes, stirring frequently. Remove from the heat and stir in the cheese, pimientos, and mustard, stirring well to combine the ingredients and melt the cheese. Serve immediately.

Play It Again: This reheats well in the microwave.

Lighter Touch: Use 2% milk.

SILKY CREAM OF CHICKEN SOUP

—Makes 4 servings—

With a rotisserie chicken in hand, it is very easy to enjoy the luscious taste and texture of a homemade cream of chicken soup. Canned cream of chicken soup is a lifesaver in recipes, but I love to make my own for a luxurious start to a special dinner or to stand alone for a simple family meal.

SPICE BLEND

3 tablespoons all-purpose flour
½ teaspoon salt
½ teaspoon white pepper
¼ teaspoon ground nutmeg

SOUP

2 tablespoons butter
1 large shallot, finely chopped (about 2 tablespoons)
2 (14½-ounce) cans fat-free less-sodium chicken broth (about 3½ cups)
2 cups bite-size chunks rotisserie chicken, skin removed (as much white meat as possible)
¾ cup heavy (whipping) cream
2 tablespoons dry vermouth
2 tablespoons finely chopped flat-leaf (Italian) parsley

1. **MAKE THE SPICE BLEND:** Stir the ingredients together in a small bowl and set aside.

2. **MAKE THE SOUP:** Melt the butter in a Dutch oven over medium heat. Add the shallot and cook, stirring frequently, until it softens, about 2 minutes. Do not brown. Sprinkle the spice blend over all and cook for 2 minutes, stirring constantly to prevent sticking.

3. Gradually whisk in the broth, stirring constantly. Do not add more broth until the mixture is smooth. Bring to a boil, then lower the heat to maintain a gentle boil. Boil, uncovered, for 5 minutes, whisking frequently and to the edge of the pot. The soup will thicken slightly.

4. Turn the heat to medium-low and stir in the chicken, cream, and vermouth. Bring to a simmer and simmer, stirring frequently, until the soup is hot and the flavors have blended, about 5 minutes. Do not boil. Sprinkle with parsley and serve.

VARIATIONS

Silky Cream of Chicken and Asparagus Soup:

Omit the parsley. Partially thaw a 10-ounce package of frozen asparagus spears. Chop into 2-inch pieces. After the soup has simmered and is ready to serve, stir in the asparagus and heat for 1 minute.

Silky Cream of Chicken and Mushroom Soup:

After the shallot is limp, add 1½ cups sliced mushrooms, button or wild, to the pan. Cook, stirring frequently, until the mushrooms begin to lose their juices, 2–3 minutes. Sprinkle with the spice blend and continue with the recipe.

WHITE BEAN AND ESCAROLE SOUP

—Makes 6–8 servings—

———— ✦ ————

This is one of my favorite fall and winter soups. It is substantial enough to be a hearty meal when paired with a crusty loaf of bread. The escarole will still have some body after simmering in the soup. Look for escarole that has a crisp texture and store tightly wrapped in the vegetable crisper for a few days.

SPICE BLEND

1 teaspoon dried thyme, crumbled between the fingers

½ teaspoon dried rosemary, crumbled between the fingers

½ teaspoon salt

¼ teaspoon pepper

1 large bay leaf

Pinch of cayenne (optional)

SOUP

3 tablespoons olive oil, divided

½ pound kielbasa, chopped into bite-size chunks

1 large onion, chopped (about 1 cup)

1 large rib celery, sliced into ¼-inch pieces (about 1 cup)

1 cup baby carrots, sliced crosswise into ¼-inch rounds

2 cups bite-size chunks rotisserie chicken

2 teaspoons jarred minced garlic

3 (14½-ounce) cans fat-free less-sodium chicken broth (about 5¼ cups)

2 (15-ounce) cans cannellini beans, undrained

4 cups coarsely chopped escarole

1. **MAKE THE SPICE BLEND:** Stir the ingredients together in a small bowl and set aside.

2. **MAKE THE SOUP:** Lightly coat a soup pot or Dutch oven with nonstick cooking spray. Add 1 tablespoon oil and warm over medium heat. Add the kielbasa and cook, stirring frequently,

until it just begins to turn brown, 3–4 minutes. Remove from the pan and set aside. Add the remaining 2 tablespoons oil to the pan, then add the onion, celery, and carrots, and cook, stirring frequently, until the vegetables begin to soften, about 4 minutes. Add the chicken, garlic, and spice blend, and cook for 2 minutes, stirring constantly. Stir in the broth and beans, raise the heat to medium-high, and bring to a boil, stirring frequently.

3. When the soup boils, turn the heat to low and simmer, uncovered, for 10 minutes, stirring frequently. Stir in the kielbasa and escarole, and simmer 5 more minutes, stirring occasionally. The escarole will not be completely soft. Remove the bay leaf and serve immediately.

▶ Notes

- Escarole is a member of the endive family.
- Add any leftover escarole to your next green salad bowl and top with chunks of rotisserie chicken and your favorite veggies. Sprinkle on some croutons and drizzle on your favorite salad dressing.

Play It Again: This reheats well.

Company's Coming: This is a pretty soup. Ladled into tureens, it is perfect for a casual company dinner.

WALK-AWAY CHICKEN SOUP

—Makes 4 servings—

A rotisserie chicken carcass or two and a trusty slow cooker team up to make a delicious chicken soup that is almost ready when you walk in the door. I prepare the ingredients and put them in the refrigerator the night before. It takes no time to start the slow cooker in the morning, and that evening homemade soup is but a few minutes away.

STOCK

1 large or 2 regular rotisserie chicken carcasses

1 large onion, cut into quarters

1 large rib celery, leaves included, cut into 4-inch pieces

1 large carrot, cut into 4-inch pieces

5–6 sprigs flat-leaf (Italian) parsley

1 large bay leaf

5 peppercorns (optional)

8 cups water

SOUP

1½ cups large shreds rotisserie chicken, pulled apart by hand

1 cup baby carrots, cut into ¼-inch rounds

1 cup wide egg noodles

½ cup medium sliced celery

1 bay leaf

1 tablespoon dried parsley flakes

1 teaspoon salt

½ teaspoon pepper

1. **MAKE THE STOCK:** Place the ingredients in a 4–5-quart slow cooker, preferably round. Cook on low for 8 hours. Do not lift the lid while the stock is cooking. Use a slotted spoon to carefully remove the solids from the slow cooker. Discard.

2. **MAKE THE SOUP:** Stir in the soup ingredients and cook on low for 45 minutes to 1 hour, until the noodles and carrots are tender. Remove the bay leaf and serve immediately.

- You can make the stock ahead and refrigerate, or freeze the cooled stock until you are ready to finish the soup. To serve, just bring the stock to a boil, add the rest of the ingredients, and cook until the carrots are tender.

Play It Again: If you do not finish the whole pot of soup remove the solids with a slotted spoon and store them separately. Otherwise, the noodles will absorb all the rich broth.

Lighter Touch: Use a paper towel to carefully blot fat from the top of stock. To eliminate more of the fat, chill the stock before adding the solids. The fat will rise to the top and solidify, and you can easily spoon it off and discard it.

"CHOCK-FULL OF GOOD STUFF" GUMBO

—Makes 4 servings—

A good pot of gumbo is a thing of culinary beauty. My rescue version, brimming with sausage, shrimp, and chunks of chicken, is a great stand-in for versions made with long-cooking flour-based roux. The rice absorbs the juices if you let this rest, so dig right in or add a splash of chicken broth when you reheat it. I like to serve corn muffins or French bread alongside this soup.

2 tablespoons vegetable oil

½ cup finely chopped green bell pepper (about ½ medium pepper)

½ cup finely chopped onion (about 1 small onion)

½ cup finely chopped celery (about 1 small rib)

3 (14½-ounce) cans fat-free less-sodium chicken broth (about 5¼ cups)

2 cups bite-size chunks rotisserie chicken

½ pound Andouille sausage or kielbasa, sliced into ¼-inch semicircles (about 1½ cups)

1 (7 to 8-ounce) package New Orleans–style gumbo mix with rice

1 bay leaf

1 cup frozen uncooked and cleaned shrimp, (about 80–90 to a pound)

1. Lightly coat a soup pot or Dutch oven with nonstick cooking spray and warm over medium heat. Add the oil and let heat for 1 minute. Add the green pepper, onion, and celery. Cook until the vegetables begin to soften, about 4 minutes, stirring frequently. Add the broth, chicken, sausage, gumbo mix, and bay leaf, and bring to a boil over medium-high heat, stirring frequently. Turn the heat to low, cover, and simmer for 10 minutes, stirring occasionally. Add the shrimp and stir well. Return to a simmer and cook covered, until the rice and shrimp are cooked and still tender, 10–15 minutes, stirring occasionally. Remove the bay leaf and serve immediately.

Feeling Flush: Drain one 6-ounce can of cleaned crabmeat and stir it in when the gumbo has finished simmering.

Company's Coming: Make a few batches and tell your friends to bring their spoons.

CREAMY WILD RICE AND LEEK SOUP

—Makes 4–6 servings—

Wild rice and leeks say autumn to me! The wild mushrooms add even more earthiness to this soothing soup. I round out the meal with a crusty loaf of bread and juicy red apple slices. Some cooks shy away from leeks because they are not sure how to clean them. Read the "Note" if you have been missing the blend of garlic and onion flavors that leeks offer. Prepare the spice and leeks while the mushrooms soak.

1 (1-ounce) package wild dried mushroom blend (porcini, oyster, shiitake, and horn of plenty), about ½ cup

SPICE BLEND

1½ teaspoons dried thyme, crumbled between the fingers
½ teaspoon salt

½ teaspoon dry mustard
½ teaspoon black pepper
¼ teaspoon ground nutmeg

SOUP

2–3 medium leeks (about 1½ pounds), tough part of green tops discarded
3 tablespoons butter
1 tablespoon olive oil
1 cup baby carrots, cut crosswise into ¼-inch rounds
1 (6-ounce) package long-grain and wild rice mix, not quick cooking (about ¾ cup), seasoning packet reserved for another use

3 (14½-ounce) cans fat-free less-sodium chicken broth (about 5¼ cups)
1 bay leaf
2 cups bite-size chunks rotisserie chicken, white and dark meat
½ cup half-and-half, at room temperature

1. Boil 1 cup water in a measuring cup in the microwave. Place the mushrooms in the water, stir, and soak until softened, 10–15 minutes.

2. **MAKE THE SPICE BLEND:** Meanwhile, stir the ingredients together in a small bowl and set aside.

3. **MAKE THE SOUP:** Clean the leeks and shake off any excess water. Place the leeks flat-side down and thinly slice crosswise. You should have about 3 cups. Heat the butter and oil in a Dutch oven over medium heat. When the butter melts, add the leeks and cook, stirring frequently, until almost tender but not brown, about 6 minutes. Add the carrots and cook, stirring frequently, until they begin to soften, about 4 minutes. Stir in the wild rice mix and the spice blend, and cook 1 minute, stirring constantly. Add the broth and bay leaf, stir well, and bring to a boil.

4. Meanwhile, use a slotted spoon to remove the mushrooms from the liquid. Set aside. Put a strainer over a cup and pour the mushroom liquid into the cup. Discard any solids in the strainer and add the liquid to the pot. Boil the soup for 5 minutes, stirring occasionally. While the soup boils, slice the mushrooms, add them to the pot along with the chicken, and stir. Turn the heat to low and simmer, covered, until the rice is tender and the flavors have melded, about 10 minutes. Stir occasionally. Stir in the half-and-half and heat through. Do not boil. Remove the bay leaf and serve.

▶ Notes

- Leeks can be very sandy, but cleaning them is as simple as one, two, three.
1. Cut the tough green leaves off the top and discard them. Leave the more tender green leaves.
2. Cut off the root ends.
3. Cut the leeks in half lengthwise and run under cold water, rinsing thoroughly until no sand appears.

> **Play It Again:** This reheats well. Remove the solids with a slotted spoon and refrigerate them separately or the rice will absorb the liquid from the soup.

ALMOST-NO-CHOPPING BLACK BEAN AND SALSA SOUP

—Makes 4 servings—

This soup is simplicity at its best. It is a great choice when you are truly pressed for time because you can put a bowl of your favorite tortilla chips on the table and let everyone crumble their own. My husband and sons absolutely love this. You will love that it is so good and requires so little effort.

3 (14½-ounce) cans fat-free less-sodium chicken broth (about 5¼ cups)

1 (16-ounce) jar chunky salsa

2½ cups rotisserie chicken shreds, meat pulled apart by hand

1 (15½-ounce) can black beans, drained and rinsed

⅔ cup instant rice

1 cup frozen corn kernels

3 green onions, thinly sliced (about ½ cup)

Tortilla chips

1. Bring the broth and salsa to a boil in a 3-quart saucepan over medium heat. Add the chicken, beans, and rice. Stir well, turn the heat to low, and simmer, covered, for 10 minutes, stirring occasionally. Stir in the corn and cook until tender, about 3 minutes. Remove from the heat and stir in the onions. Ladle into soup bowls and serve immediately, breaking tortilla chips on top.

SCRUMPTIOUS STEWS

These great recipes deliver flavor in a flash. When we think of stews, we often think of pots that simmer for hours before you can eat. Not so with the flavorful addition of a rotisserie chicken. A hearty bowl of delicious homemade stew or chili can be yours in no time flat. I jump-start the flavor by including a handpicked selection of ingredients and by incorporating quick flavor-building techniques, such as warming the spices.

The cooking times are short with these recipes, but the results are every bit as good as their long-simmering cousins. Like almost all stews, these can be made in advance and reheated. With dishes like Brunswick Stew and Sweet Potato, Coconut Milk, and Banana Curry to choose from, you will put a warming stew on your table much more frequently.

NO-TIME-FLAT CHICKEN CHILI

—Makes 6 servings—

There are a lot of ingredients in this dish, and each brings its own flavor, a quick stand-in for hours of simmering. The rotisserie chicken and kidney and pinto beans make a substantial combination. Serve as is or over rice, which my family often does. Ready-to-bake refrigerated corn biscuits and a green salad alongside can round out the scrumptious meal.

SPICE BLEND

¼ cup mild chili powder

1 tablespoon ground cumin

2 tablespoons dried oregano, crumbled between the fingers

1 teaspoon salt

CHILI

2 tablespoons vegetable oil

1 large onion, chopped (about 1 cup)

1 large green bell pepper, chopped (about 1 cup)

1 (7-ounce) can diced mild chiles, undrained

1 (6-ounce) can tomato paste

1 tablespoon jarred minced garlic

3 cups rotisserie chicken chunks, meat pulled apart by hand

1 (28-ounce) can crushed tomatoes in purée

1 can *each* (about 15-ounces each) kidney beans and pinto beans, undrained

1 (14½-ounce) can fat-free less-sodium chicken broth (about 1¾ cups)

½ cup finely chopped cilantro

1. **MAKE THE SPICE BLEND:** Mix the ingredients together in a small bowl and set aside.

2. **MAKE THE CHILI:** Lightly coat a Dutch oven with nonstick cooking spray. Heat the oil in the pan over medium-high heat. Add the onion and bell pepper, and cook, stirring frequently,

until they begin to soften, about 4 minutes. Lower the heat to medium, add chiles, tomato paste, garlic, and spice blend, and cook for 2 minutes, stirring constantly. Add the chicken, tomatoes, beans, and broth, stir well and bring to a boil, stirring frequently. Turn the heat to low and simmer, covered, for 15 minutes, stirring frequently. Stir in the cilantro and serve.

▶ **Notes**

- Chili powders are blends of spices, so try different brands to find the ones you like.
- The spices in this dish are double-developed: once when they cook with the onion, pepper, chiles, and tomato paste, and again when they simmer away in the pot.

Lighter Touch: The beans, tomatoes, and chicken put this on my "good-for-you" list.

Play It Again: Leftover chili pairs with a 28-ounce tube of polenta to make a great chili pie. Lightly coat an 8 × 8-inch baking pan with nonstick cooking spray. Pour about 3 cups of chili into the pan. Top with 1/2-inch-thick slices of polenta and sprinkle with 2 cups already-shredded Cheddar cheese. Bake in a 350° F oven until the filling is bubbly and the cheese melts.

Company's Coming: Make two batches and invite friends over with confidence.

BRUNSWICK STEW

Makes 6–8 servings

This is my rescue version of a true southern classic. Southerners feel strongly about Brunswick stew. Traditionally made with squirrel many years ago, this hearty vegetable-rich dish is just terrific with the more readily available rotisserie chicken.

SPICE BLEND

2 teaspoons dried thyme, crumbled between the fingers
½ teaspoon salt
¼ teaspoon cayenne

BASE

1 large rotisserie chicken (about 32 ounces)
4 slices bacon
1 large onion, chopped (about 1 cup)
1 large green bell pepper, chopped (about 1 cup)

1 (6-ounce) can tomato paste
3 tablespoons Worcestershire sauce
1 tablespoon jarred minced garlic

VEGETABLES

2 (14½-ounce) cans fat-free less-sodium chicken broth (about 3½ cups)
1 (28-ounce) can diced tomatoes in juice
2 cups frozen lima beans

1½ cups frozen corn kernels
1 large bay leaf
1 (14½-ounce can) sliced potatoes, drained (about 1¾ cups)

1. **MAKE THE SPICE BLEND:** Stir the ingredients together in a small bowl and set aside.

2. **MAKE THE BASE:** Pull the chicken meat from the bone in large bite-size pieces. You should have 3–4 cups. Set aside. Cook the bacon until crisp in a large Dutch oven over medium heat, stirring frequently. Place the bacon on a paper-towel-lined plate, leaving the drippings in the pan.

3. Raise the heat to medium-high. Add the onion and bell pepper to the pan with the bacon drippings and cook, stirring frequently, until they have softened, 4–6 minutes. Lower the heat to medium. Add the tomato paste, Worcestershire sauce, garlic, and spice blend and cook for 1 minute, stirring constantly.

4. **ADD THE VEGETABLES:** Add the broth, tomatoes, reserved chicken, lima beans, corn, and bay leaf. Stir well and bring just to a boil. Simmer, uncovered, until the mixture has thickened slightly and the lima beans are tender, about 10 minutes. Stir frequently to prevent sticking. Add the potatoes and stir, breaking up the potatoes with the spoon. Simmer for 5 minutes, then take off the heat. Remove the bay leaf and discard. Crumble the bacon into pieces and stir into the pot. Serve immediately.

▶ Note
- I like to serve skillet-baked corn bread alongside.

ROASTED CHICKEN RATATOUILLE

—Makes 4 servings—

A rotisserie chicken quickly transforms a classic Provençal side dish into a main course. A pleasing dinner when offered with a crusty loaf of bread and a glass of wine, it is also a great way to slip in different vegetables for the reluctant diner. I leave the skin on the eggplant for texture and color, and as a time-saving technique. This is wonderful served as is or over pasta.

SPICE BLEND

½ teaspoon dried Italian herb seasoning, crumbled between the fingers
½ teaspoon paprika

½ teaspoon salt
½ teaspoon pepper

BASE

¼ cup olive oil, divided
1 large onion, thinly sliced (about 1 cup)
1 small eggplant (about 8 ounces), with peel on and cut into ½-inch cubes (about 2 cups)
1 large red bell pepper, chopped (about 1 cup)
1 cup sliced mushrooms
1 tablespoon jarred minced garlic

2 small zucchini, sliced ¼-inch thick (about 1 cup)
2 cups bite-size chunks rotisserie chicken
1 (28-ounce) can diced tomatoes in juice
1 bay leaf
3 tablespoons finely chopped flat-leaf (Italian) parsley
½ cup already-shredded Parmesan cheese (optional)

1. **MAKE THE SPICE BLEND:** Stir the ingredients together in a small bowl and set aside.

2. **MAKE THE BASE:** Heat 2 tablespoons of the oil in a Dutch oven over medium-high heat. Add the onion and cook, stirring frequently, until it begins to soften, about 4 minutes. Add the remaining 2 tablespoons of oil along with the eggplant, bell pepper, mushrooms, and garlic. Sprinkle with the spice blend and cook, stirring frequently, until the vegetables begin to soften, about 4 minutes. Add the zucchini and cook for 2 minutes, stirring frequently. Add the chicken and cook 2 more minutes, stirring frequently.

3. Add the tomatoes and bay leaf, and bring to a boil, stirring frequently. Turn the heat to low, cover, and simmer for 15 minutes, stirring frequently to prevent sticking. Remove from the heat and stir in the parsley. Remove the bay leaf and discard. Serve immediately, sprinkling cheese over each serving, if desired.

▶ Note

- This is a superb do-ahead dish. The flavors are even better the next day. Reheat in the microwave just until hot.

Play It Again: If the weather is warm, treat yourself to leftovers as a nice cold salad.

SWEET POTATO, COCONUT MILK, AND BANANA CURRY

—Makes 4 servings—

This stew has evolved since my college days when I first experimented with coconut milk and curry. Hearty and mildly spicy with a touch of sweetness, this is ideal for kids and adults alike. Canned sweet potatoes also come packed with brown sugar and spices. Be careful not to buy that variety for this stew.

SPICE BLEND

2 tablespoons mild curry powder
½ teaspoon salt
¼ teaspoon ground allspice
¼ teaspoon ground cinnamon
Cayenne, to taste

STEW

2 tablespoons vegetable oil
2 cups thinly sliced onion semicircles (about 2 large or 1 extra-large)
1 large red bell pepper, chopped (about 1 cup)
1 tablespoon jarred chopped ginger
2 teaspoons jarred minced garlic
2 (15-ounce) cans sweet potatoes packed in light syrup, drained, and cut into ½-inch cubes
½ cup fat-free less-sodium chicken broth
¾ cup water
2½ cups chopped rotisserie chicken chunks
1 (14-ounce) can coconut milk, not sweetened
⅔ cup raisins
1 large or 2 medium ripe but firm bananas
Hot jasmine rice

1. **MAKE THE SPICE BLEND:** Stir the ingredients together in a small bowl and set aside.

2. **MAKE THE STEW:** Lightly coat a Dutch oven or soup pot with nonstick cooking spray. Heat the oil in the pan over medium heat. Add the onion and cook, stirring frequently, until it just begins to soften, about 4 minutes. Add the bell pepper, ginger, and garlic, and cook, stirring frequently, until the pepper begins to soften, about 4 minutes. Sprinkle the spice blend over all and cook for 2 minutes, stirring constantly.

3. Add the sweet potatoes to the pot along with the broth and water. Bring to a boil, turn the heat to medium-low, and stir in the chicken, coconut milk, and raisins. Simmer for 10 minutes, stirring frequently. Meanwhile, cut the bananas crosswise into $\frac{1}{2}$-inch rounds. You should have about 1 cup. Stir in the bananas and simmer 5 more minutes, stirring frequently. Serve over the hot rice.

Company's Coming: This hearty curry is luscious enough for company. The jasmine rice adds to the exotic flavor.

Do-Ahead Tip: You can make this a day in advance. Just wait until serving time to add the bananas. Stir them in when the stew warms up and then simmer about 5 minutes.

CAMPFIRE BAKED BEAN STEW

—Makes about 4 servings—

Kids dig right into this simple add-and-stir dish that is reminiscent of one of the meals we cooked over the campfire at Girl Scout camp. Adults with a nostalgic taste for sweet and savory will also enjoy it. Serve with corn muffins or bake some refrigerated corn biscuits to serve alongside.

1 (28-ounce) can original-style baked beans with bacon and brown sugar
2 cups bite-size chunks rotisserie chicken
1½ cups canned French-fried onions
1 (10¾-ounce) can tomato soup, undiluted
½ cup frozen corn kernels

¼ cup firmly packed brown sugar
2 tablespoons ketchup
1 tablespoon Dijon mustard
6 slices bacon, cooked and crumbled
Garnish: already-shredded Cheddar cheese and ½ bunch green onions, sliced

1. Combine all the ingredients except the bacon and garnish in a Dutch oven. Add half a soup can of water and bring the mixture to a simmer over medium heat, stirring occasionally. Turn the heat to low and simmer, covered, for 15 minutes, stirring frequently to prevent sticking. Stir in the bacon and simmer 5 more minutes, stirring frequently. Sprinkle with cheese and onions as desired.

▶ Note
   • The French-fried onions give a good onion flavor, and you don't have to touch a knife.

Company's Coming: Great playdate fare.

GREEK CHICKEN STEW

With bottled Greek seasoning and a rotisserie chicken, you can spoil your family with the delights of a Greek dinner unbelievably quickly. The couscous adds a nice medley of flavors and really makes this stew come alive.

3 tablespoons olive oil

1 large onion, chopped (about 1 cup)

1 large green bell pepper, chopped (about 1 cup)

1 tablespoon jarred minced garlic

4 teaspoons dried Greek seasoning, crumbled between the fingers

1 (28-ounce) can crushed tomatoes in purée

1 (15-ounce) can garbanzo beans, rinsed and drained

1 cup fat-free less-sodium chicken broth

2 bay leaves

Pepper, to taste

1 rotisserie chicken, cut into serving pieces

½ cup pitted kalamata olives, coarsely chopped

1 tablespoon freshly-squeezed lemon juice

Cinnamon Couscous (recipe follows)

1. Heat the oil in a Dutch oven over medium-high heat. Add the onion and bell pepper, and cook, stirring frequently, until they begin to soften, about 4 minutes. Add the garlic and seasoning and cook for 1 minute, stirring constantly. Add the tomatoes, garbanzo beans, broth, bay leaves, and pepper. Stir well. Bring to a boil and boil for 5 minutes, stirring frequently. Add the chicken, lower the heat to medium, and simmer, uncovered, for 15 minutes. Stir frequently to prevent sticking. The mixture will thicken. Remove the bay leaves and discard. Stir in the olives and lemon juice, and serve immediately over the couscous.

CINNAMON COUSCOUS

—Makes about 5¼ cups—

2 cups fat-free less-sodium chicken broth or
  1 (14½ ounce) can fat-free less-sodium
  chicken broth plus ¼ cup water
1 tablespoon olive oil
½ teaspoon salt

1 (10-ounce) box plain, quick-cooking
  couscous (about 1⅓ cups)
¼ cup raisins
1 teaspoon ground cinnamon
1 tablespoon orange juice

1. While the stew is simmering, bring the broth, oil, and salt to a boil in a medium saucepan over medium-high heat. Stir in the couscous and raisins, cover, and remove the pan from the heat. When the moisture has been absorbed, about 5 minutes, sprinkle the cinnamon and orange juice over the couscous. Fluff with a fork to combine the flavors and loosen the couscous. Do not stir.

TOMATILLO POSOLE

—Makes 4 servings—

—✦—

This robust soup-stew is my posole version of my friend Phyllis's tomatillo chili. Posole refers both to the garbanzo bean–size corn kernels called hominy and the Mexican stew traditionally studded with pork and hominy. The garnishes add the color, flavor, and textures of a fresh salad to the warm bowls of satisfying stew. What a treat!

SPICE BLEND

5 teaspoons chili powder
1 teaspoon ground cumin
½ teaspoon salt

STEW

3 tablespoons vegetable oil
1 large onion, sliced in half lengthwise then thinly sliced crosswise (about 1 cup)
1 (4-ounce) can mild diced green chiles, drained, or 1 tablespoon canned diced jalapeño peppers
1 tablespoon jarred minced garlic
1 tablespoon chopped shallot (optional)

2½ cups large shreds rotisserie chicken, pulled apart by hand
2 (15-ounce) cans or 1 (30-ounce) can hominy, drained
2 (14½-ounce) cans fat-free less-sodium chicken broth (about 3½ cups)
1 (16-ounce) jar chunky salsa verde (green salsa)

ACCOMPANIMENTS

Shredded iceberg lettuce, chopped cilantro, chopped avocado, chopped tomatoes, and sliced green onion
Lime wedges

1. **MAKE THE SPICE BLEND:** Stir the ingredients together in a small bowl and set aside.

2. **MAKE THE STEW:** Heat the oil in a Dutch oven or soup pot over medium heat. Add the onion and cook, stirring frequently, until it begins to soften, about 4 minutes. Add the chiles, garlic, and shallot, if using, and cook 2 more minutes, stirring constantly. Add the chicken, sprinkle in the spice blend, and cook for 2 minutes, stirring constantly. Add the hominy and broth, raise the heat to high, and bring to a boil, stirring occasionally. Turn the heat to low and simmer, covered, for 10 minutes, stirring frequently. Stir in the salsa and simmer, covered, 5 more minutes, stirring occasionally.

3. Ladle into serving bowls. Top with accompaniments, as desired, and squeeze a little lime juice over all.

▶ Notes

- You can substitute ancho chili powder for 2 teaspoons of the chili powder if you happen to have it on hand. It adds a nice depth of flavor.
- Check the label to make sure the salsa has tomatillos, also known as Mexican green tomatoes. Their acidic kick is key to this dish.

Play It Again: Simmer the leftovers long enough to cook away most of the liquid, then roll everything up in a large flour tortilla. Sprinkle with garnishes and a little shredded cheese for a great burrito.

Company's Coming: Serve with corn muffins or tortillas for great get-together fare.

QUICK CASSOULET

Makes about 8 servings

I fell in love with cassoulet years ago when, eyes glued to the television screen, I watched Julia Child tend to the bubbling pot that contained all manner of beans, poultry, and sausages destined to simmer for hours. I joyfully made it that way for years. These days I reach into my rotisserie chicken pantry and stir up my delicious streamlined cassoulet. It offers all the rich aromas and earthy comfort I love in a cassoulet in a time frame I can manage. Do not be put off by the long ingredient list; most of this is pour and stir. Serve with crusty bread and a salad of bitter greens.

SPICE BLEND

1 teaspoon dried thyme, crumbled between the fingers
1 teaspoon salt, or to taste

½ teaspoon pepper
Pinch of cloves (optional)

CRUST

1 cup dried unseasoned bread crumbs
2 teaspoons olive oil

BEAN MIXTURE

6 slices cold bacon, coarsely chopped

8 ounces baby carrots (about 1¾ cups), cut crosswise into fourths

1 medium onion, cut in half and sliced crosswise into ¼-inch pieces

1 pound kielbasa, sliced into ½-inch rounds

1 tablespoon jarred minced garlic

3 cups large chunks rotisserie chicken plus container juices, meat pulled apart by hand

2 (15-ounce) cans white kidney beans (cannelini), undrained

1 (15-ounce) can small white beans, undrained

1 (14½-ounce) can diced tomatoes in juice

1 (14½-ounce) can fat-free less-sodium chicken broth (about 1¾ cups)

½ cup dry white wine or vermouth

2 bay leaves

1. **MAKE THE SPICE BLEND:** Stir the ingredients together in a small bowl and set aside.

2. **MAKE THE CRUST:** Lightly coat a 5–6 quart Dutch oven with nonstick cooking spray and place over medium heat. Add the bread crumbs and oil, and stir well to combine. Cook until the crumbs are crispy and have turned a golden brown, about 3 minutes. Stir constantly to brown evenly and avoid burning; do not walk away. Remove from the heat and immediately spoon into a bowl. Set aside. Carefully wipe the pan clean with a dry paper towel.

3. **MAKE THE BEAN MIXTURE:** Cook the bacon in the Dutch oven over medium heat until crisp, stirring frequently. Remove with a slotted spoon and drain on a paper-towel-lined plate, leaving the drippings in the pan. Increase the heat to medium-high, add the carrots to the pan, and cook for 2 minutes, stirring constantly. Add the onion and kielbasa, and cook until the onion turns golden and the kielbasa begins to brown, about 8 minutes, stirring frequently. Add the spice blend and garlic, and cook for 2 minutes, stirring constantly.

4. Add the chicken, container juices, beans, tomatoes, broth, wine, and bay leaves. Stir thoroughly but gently to combine. Raise the heat to high and bring to a full boil, stirring occasionally. Boil, uncovered, for 3 minutes, stirring frequently to prevent sticking. Turn the heat to low and stir the bacon into the pot. Simmer, covered, for 10 minutes to blend the flavors, stirring frequently to prevent sticking. Remove the bay leaves and discard. Ladle into bowls and sprinkle lightly with the toasted bread crumbs.

▶ Notes

- Bacon chops more easily when it is cold, so chop the bacon right after you take it out of the refrigerator. If the bacon warms up it will move around on the cutting board.
- Long cooking breaks down beans, giving them a nice creamy texture. I use one can of small white beans along with the traditional larger beans because the smaller beans break down faster, giving my quick cassoulet some of the creaminess of its long-simmering cousin.

Lighter Touch: Traditionally rich with goose or duck fat, this version is already lighter than the norm with none of that fat and less than one slice of bacon per serving. If you want to make this even lighter, use 3 slices of bacon and a reduced-fat sausage. Add 1 tablespoon of olive oil to the bacon drippings before cooking the carrots.

Do-Ahead Tip: This is great do-ahead dining, perfect for at-home parties or potlucks. Make two to three batches for a big get-together. Refrigerate for a day or two, or freeze for up to two weeks in quart-size containers or plastic freezer bags.

Play It Again: This recipe makes a generous number of servings, but do not worry about leftovers because it reheats and freezes well.

SAY SANDWICH

Rotisserie chicken and sandwiches are a match made in culinary heaven. Years ago the only bread we could find in the market was spongy white bread, and our spread choices were mustard and mayonnaise. Not so anymore. Our culinary world has reached out to include tortillas and pita bread as wrappers and everything from yogurt to pesto as spreads. You can use prebaked pizza crusts to get a rotisserie chicken pizza to the table faster than the delivery boy can get to your door.

When you think rotisserie chickens and sandwiches, think choices. Use the recipes in this chapter as springboards for ideas, but do not let them limit you. Sometimes rotisserie chicken can step in for the usual meat, as in my Rotisserie Reuben where chicken replaces the typical corned beef. Other times you can pull together ingredients that you have on hand to whip up a quick sandwich, like the Three Pepper Hero.

The ever-popular wrap sandwiches use tortillas as the bread. Plain flour tortillas are great, but look for flavored tortillas—spinach, sun-dried tomato, or herb—to start your sandwich out with more flavor. Chunked or shredded chicken and anything from roasted red peppers to brown rice and broccoli can fill out the sandwich. Drizzle on your favorite bottled dressing, and you are ready to eat. If you are in the mood for a chicken Caesar wrap, pop open the bag of Caesar salad mix found in the produce section, divide it among as many tortillas as you like, add the chunks of rotisserie chicken, and drizzle on the packaged dressing. It doesn't get any easier. For a lunch to go, pack the ingredients separately and assemble the sandwich when you are ready to eat.

Just remember that most sandwiches are made of bread, spread, poultry or meat, maybe some cheese, and some veggies. From there your imagination is your only limit. Try different cheeses from the deli case, such as Havarti and fontina. Add a sliced pear to a simple grilled chicken and cheese sandwich for a different touch. Or wrap your sandwich in a lettuce leaf or a rice paper wrapper if you have them. I am sure that the recipes in this chapter, combined with the wide range of breads and the infinite possibilities from a rotisserie chicken, will help you create many terrific sandwiches.

ALL-AMERICAN WRAP

—Makes 2 servings—

Quick and crunchy, this sandwich is a great way to pile on the veggies with just a little bit of effort. The celery seed and mustard bring a true slaw flavor in no time at all. Eat this right after you make it since it gets soggy if you let it sit.

COLESLAW

1½ cups packaged coleslaw mix
¼ cup reduced-fat mayonnaise
2 teaspoons freshly-squeezed lemon juice
1 teaspoon cider vinegar
1 teaspoon mustard, Dijon or yellow

1 teaspoon celery seed
⅛ teaspoon *each* garlic powder and onion powder
Salt and pepper, to taste

SANDWICH

1 large burrito-size flour tortilla (about 10 inches across), or 2 soft taco–size flour tortillas
2 slices ready-to-serve bacon, warmed according to package directions and crumbled

¾–1 cup chopped rotisserie chicken
1 small tomato, chopped

1. **MAKE THE COLESLAW:** Stir the ingredients together in a medium bowl.

2. **MAKE THE SANDWICH.** Put the tortilla on a flat surface and spread with the coleslaw, leaving a ½-inch border. Sprinkle the bacon down the middle of the coleslaw. Top with the chicken and tomatoes. Roll into a cylinder, cut on the diagonal, and serve.

▶ Notes

- Use one of the flavored tortillas if you are in the mood.
- This recipe doubles well. Just use 1½ teaspoons of celery seed and twice as much of everything else.

In a Pinch: Substitute about 1 cup deli coleslaw for the homemade version and use about 4 tablespoons jarred real bacon bits for the bacon.

CHICKEN "GYROS"

—Makes 4 servings—

I wrap warm, tender slices of marinated rotisserie chicken breast in a soft pita round and then top with a creamy yogurt-based sauce and the traditional accompaniments to treat myself to a lighter version of the popular lamb sandwich. Remove the breast from the chicken whole, peel away the skin, and then slice. Don't let the long list of ingredients fool you. These go together in a snap.

SAUCE

¼ cup plain yogurt
¼ cup finely chopped cucumber
2 tablespoons light sour cream
1 teaspoon jarred minced garlic

1 teaspoon freshly-squeezed lemon juice
½ teaspoon dried dill weed, crumbled
   between the fingers
Salt and pepper, to taste

MARINADE

¼ cup olive oil
2 tablespoons freshly-squeezed lemon juice
2 teaspoons jarred minced garlic
1 teaspoon dried oregano, crumbled between
   the fingers

½ teaspoon ground cumin
½ teaspoon onion powder
Pinch of salt
8 (½-inch thick) lengthwise slices rotisserie
   chicken breast, skin removed

SANDWICHES

4 pita rounds (each about 6 inches across)
4 thin slices red onion, divided into rings

About 1 cup torn romaine lettuce leaves
1 large tomato, chopped

1. **MAKE THE SAUCE:** Stir the sauce ingredients together in a medium bowl. Set aside.

2. **MAKE THE MARINADE:** Combine all the ingredients except the chicken in a 12-inch non-stick skillet. Stir together. Place the chicken slices flat in the skillet and spoon the marinade over the top.

3. **MAKE THE SANDWICHES:** Heat the skillet over medium heat. Cook the chicken slices until they just begin to brown on one side, about 4 minutes. Carefully turn them over and brown lightly on the other side, about 2 minutes longer. Remove to a plate. Stack the pita rounds, wrap in damp paper towels, and microwave on high power for 30 seconds. Do not split the pitas. Distribute the chicken slices among the pita rounds. Top with onion, lettuce, and tomato, dividing evenly among the rounds. Spoon the sauce on top, fold over, and serve.

▶ Notes

- The sauce for this sandwich is my version of the classic Greek sauce tzatziki. I find the cucumber seeds refreshing, but you can certainly remove them if you prefer. Double the recipe if you like a lot of sauce.
- Let the kids stir the sauce and put the toppings on the sandwiches.

In a Pinch: Substitute a generous ⅓ cup of bottled Greek salad dressing for the marinade if you are truly pressed for time.

Just You or Two: Simply cut the sandwich recipe in half for two of you. Use the extra sauce as a dip.

CHEDDAR AND BACON MUFFIN MELTS

—Makes 4 open-face sandwiches—

———— 🥄🍴 ————

Pair a steaming hot bowl of soup or a salad with these savory muffin melts for a quick lunch or light supper. Choose a sourdough English muffin for more tang, and pan fry your favorite specialty bacon if you have more time. Lightly toast the English muffin halves as the broiler preheats, then assemble the sandwiches.

SPICE BLEND

½ teaspoon paprika
Pinch of salt
Pinch of pepper

SANDWICHES

2 English muffins, split in half and lightly
   toasted
Dijon mustard, to taste
2 small tomatoes, sliced
Thinly sliced rotisserie chicken breast to
   generously cover each muffin half

4 thin slices red onion
4 slices sharp Cheddar cheese (about 1 ounce
   each)
6 slices ready-to-serve bacon, broken in half
   crosswise

1. Preheat the broiler.

2. **MAKE THE SPICE BLEND:** Stir the ingredients together in a small bowl and set aside.

3. **MAKE THE SANDWICHES:** Place the toasted muffin halves on a baking sheet. Spread with mustard and top with the tomato slices. Divide the chicken slices among the muffin halves, sprinkle with the spice blend, and top with the onion slices. Cover with the cheese. Place one

slice of bacon down the center of each muffin then make an X on top of the cheese with two more slices. Broil until the cheese melts and the bacon browns, 3–5 minutes. Serve immediately.

▶ Note

- Children can easily put these together. Have them wash their hands after they handle the onions so they do not rub onion juice into their eyes.

Lighter Touch: Choose a reduced-fat Cheddar.

Just You or Two: Easy to cut down for one.

PESTO AND VEGETABLE FOCACCIA

Makes 4–6 servings

Focaccia, the often-dimpled Italian bread, makes quite a nice sandwich. Use a long serrated knife to slice the loaf in half across the middle, making a top and a bottom. The combination of pesto, chicken, and oven-roasted vegetables is rich in flavor and takes very little effort.

VEGETABLES

1 large tomato, cut into ¼-inch slices
1½ cups sliced mushrooms
4 slices red onion, each about ⅛-inch thick
3 tablespoons olive oil

1 teaspoon dried Italian herb seasoning, crumbled between the fingers
Salt and pepper, to taste

SANDWICH

1 piece focaccia (about 9 × 7½ inches), sliced in half horizontally
Refrigerated pesto sauce (about ⅓ cup)

Thinly sliced rotisserie chicken breast to cover bread

1. **PREPARE THE VEGETABLES:** Preheat the oven to 425° F. Lightly coat a 13 × 9-inch pan with nonstick cooking spray. Put the vegetables in the pan, drizzle with the oil, and sprinkle with the Italian seasoning, salt, and pepper. Stir well. Bake, stirring occasionally, until the onions are slightly tender to the bite, about 20 minutes. Remove from the oven.

2. **MAKE THE SANDWICH:** Spread the cut surfaces of the focaccia with pesto. Put half of the roasted vegetables on the bottom of the bread and top with the chicken, then the other half of the vegetables. Place the other slice of bread on top, pressing down lightly. Cut into desired pieces and serve.

▶ Notes

- Look for focaccia in the bakery at your supermarket. You may find round or rectangular shapes, and flavors ranging from garlic to sun-dried tomato. Experiment. You cannot go wrong.
- If you like, spread the bread with the pesto sauce and toast it while the oven is preheating.

Just You or Two: Cut the recipe in half and use an 8 × 8-inch pan to roast the vegetables.

Company's Coming: This travels well to picnics.

CHIPOTLE CHICKEN CLUB SANDWICH

—Makes 2 sandwiches—

This tasty twist on the conventional club sandwich comes alive when you stir smoky, spicy-hot chipotle peppers in adobo sauce into your favorite mayonnaise. Look for these canned, smoked jalapeño peppers in the Mexican food section of the market. These delicious sandwiches are perfect for lunch or a light dinner. Two slices of bread instead of the traditional three make them easy to eat without sacrificing a bit of flavor.

CHIPOTLE SPREAD

½ cup mayonnaise
2 teaspoons finely chopped chipotle peppers
   in adobo sauce, or to taste
2 medium cloves garlic, minced (about
   1 teaspoon)

¼ teaspoon freshly-squeezed lime juice
Pinch of salt

SANDWICH

4 slices white sandwich bread, toasted
Thinly sliced rotisserie chicken breast to cover
   2 slices of bread, skin removed

6 slices bacon, cooked crisp
1 medium tomato, thinly sliced
2 crisp iceberg lettuce leaves

1. **MAKE THE SPREAD:** Stir the ingredients together in a bowl.

2. **MAKE THE SANDWICHES:** Coat each slice of toast with the chipotle spread, to taste. You may have some left over. Divide the slices of chicken between 2 slices of toast, placing the slices in a single layer on top of the spread. Top with the bacon slices and a single layer of tomato slices. Cover with the lettuce leaves and then the remaining slices of toast, spread side down.

3. Press the tops of the sandwiches down firmly. Using a serrated knife, cut through the sandwiches on the diagonal, then cut through on the diagonal in the opposite direction. Each sandwich will have 4 wedges. Place a toothpick in each of the wedges and serve.

▶ **Notes**

- Sandwiches are about proportion, not precision. Do not fret over how much chicken and how much spread to use. Let the size of the bread and your stomach be your guide.
- Leftover chipotle peppers will keep for one month in a covered glass container in the refrigerator. Freeze for longer storage. Unused chipotle spread will keep in the refrigerator for about one week.

Serve It Up: Although these are great alone or with a few tortilla chips, you can round out this satisfying meal with a quick side salad. Measure equal amounts of drained and rinsed canned black beans and thawed frozen corn kernels, and stir in salsa. Offer mango slices or mango sorbet for dessert.

In a Pinch:

- I prefer fresh garlic in this sandwich, but jarred minced garlic will work.
- Homemade chipotle spread is quick and terrific but you can buy ready-to-eat chipotle mayonnaise in the supermarket if time is truly tight.
- Save even more time by using precooked bacon slices and warming them slightly.

Double Duty: This recipe doubles well if you happen to have guests.

BROCCOLI AND CREAM CHEESE POCKETS

—Makes 8 pockets—

No need to head to the freezer case when the kids want a pocket treat. You can quickly whip up satisfying homemade stuffed pockets with the help of a rotisserie chicken, a few vegetables, and refrigerated crescent dough. Bake and fill these the day you are going to eat them. Serve with fresh fruit.

1½ cups frozen chopped broccoli, thawed

1 cup chopped rotisserie chicken, skin removed

1 (8-ounce) container whipped cream cheese, at room temperature

1 (2-ounce) jar diced pimentos, drained (about ¼ cup)

½ small onion, finely chopped (about ¼ cup)

1 teaspoon paprika

½ teaspoon jarred minced garlic

¼ teaspoon salt

¼ teaspoon ground nutmeg

2 (8-ounce) cans refrigerated crescent dinner rolls, cold

1. Position a rack in the bottom third of the oven and another rack in the center of the oven. Preheat the oven to 350° F. Line two baking sheets with aluminum foil, shiny side down.

2. Stir all the ingredients except the crescent rolls together in a small bowl.

3. Open 1 can of crescent rolls on a work surface. Divide the rolls into four rectangles, pressing each pair of triangles together to seal the perforations. Mound about ⅓ cup of the filling crosswise a little to one side of the center of the dough, forming a rectangle approximately 2¼-inches wide by 2½-inches long, leaving about a ¼-inch border. Fold the dough over crosswise to form a rectangle, then press the edges together. Press the tines of a fork along the edges to seal. Place on a baking sheet, making sure the rolls do not touch. Repeat with the remaining rolls.

4. Repeat with the remaining dough. Bake until golden brown, about 18 minutes. Switch the sheets from top to bottom after 10 minutes. Remove from the baking sheets and cool on wire racks.

▶ Notes

- These are a great way to make a fun picnic in a hurry. They travel well in a single layer and taste just great at room temperature.
- Call the kids into the kitchen. They can stir the filling and help fill and shape the dough. If the weather will not allow an outdoor picnic, spread a blanket on the floor and let the little ones enjoy an indoor picnic instead.

Turnover Tips: Do not overfill the dough, and seal it well all the way around and you will have no problems.

Lighter Touch: Choose reduced-fat crescent rolls.

BUSY DAY BURRITOS

—Makes 4–6 burritos—

These burritos are as quick as fold and roll, just what we all need at the end of a busy day. This makes four burritos if you like a hefty amount of filling; otherwise it makes more. I stir the chicken chunks and beans into the hot rice to save a step and warm everything without washing another pot. You will whip these up again and again.

RICE

1 cup instant white or brown rice
½ teaspoon salt
2½ cups large chunks rotisserie chicken, meat pulled apart by hand

1 (16-ounce) jar salsa, not chunky
1 (15-ounce) can black beans, drained and rinsed
2 teaspoons chili powder

BURRITOS

4–6 burrito-size flour tortillas (about 10-inches across), warmed according to package directions
Already-shredded Mexican-blend cheese, to taste

4 green onions, thinly sliced
Packaged torn romaine leaves
2 large tomatoes, chopped

TOPPINGS (OPTIONAL)

Light sour cream
Prepared guacamole

1. **MAKE THE RICE:** Cook the rice in a large pot according to package directions, using ½ teaspoon salt. When the rice is cooked, immediately stir in the remaining ingredients. Cook over low heat for 2 minutes, stirring constantly. Cover and remove from the heat.

2. **MAKE THE BURRITOS:** Stack the tortillas between damp paper towels and microwave on high for 30 seconds. Place the tortillas on serving plates. Divide the rice mixture among the tortillas, placing mounds in the center of the tortillas. Leave about a 2-inch border on the top and bottom. Top with cheese. Sprinkle the onions, romaine, and tomatoes over the top, dividing them evenly among the burritos.

3. Bring the bottom of the tortillas up over the mixture. Give the burritos a quarter turn so that the fold is on the right, then roll the burrito from bottom to top to form a cylinder. The top will be open. Serve immediately. Spoon optional toppings on the top or into the burritos.

▶ Note
- Older children can put these together. Let younger ones sprinkle on the toppings.

Play It Again: Reheat any leftover filling the next day and roll for a quick lunch.

BARBECUE CHICKEN PIZZA

—Makes 1 pizza (about 11-inches)—

My family loves this homemade version of the popular pizza chain's barbecue chicken pizza. The creamy Gouda and crisp red onions give a nice balance to the sweetness of the barbecue sauce. Almost faster than from the freezer with the plus of homemade taste, this gem is sure to become a family favorite.

1 large prebaked regular pizza crust
½ cup thinly sliced red onion semicircles
1½ cups bite-size chunks rotisserie chicken, skin removed
½ cup bottled barbecue sauce

½–1 cup shredded Gouda cheese
½–1 cup already-shredded mozzarella cheese
2 tablespoons finely chopped cilantro

1. Position a rack in the center of the oven and preheat the oven to 450° F. Separate the onion into individual rings and place them on the crust, leaving about a ½-inch border around the edges. Stir the chicken and barbecue sauce together in a small bowl. Spread on the crust, again leaving about a ½-inch border. Combine the cheeses and sprinkle over the chicken topping.

2. Place the pizza directly on the rack and bake until the cheese is bubbly, 12–15 minutes. Remove from the oven and sprinkle with the cilantro. Cut into wedges and serve.

▶ Notes

- How much cheese you put on a pizza is largely a matter of preference and how you feel that day. I give a range for the cheese so you can decide how much to sprinkle on.
- If you happen to have a pizza stone, just follow the manufacturer's instructions.

In a Pinch: If you don't have Gouda, substitute provolone or use all mozzarella.

Lighter Touch: Choose a thin crust to eliminate some of the bread calories.

Company's Coming: You can increase this recipe to serve as many as you need, making it a great party-time pick. Buy individual-size prebaked crusts and put out bowls of sliced onion and shredded cheeses. Stir up a big batch of the chicken topping and let guests have fun making their own individual pizzas.

CHICKEN TACOS

—Makes 4 servings—

Tacos are a mainstay in our house, so I am always on the lookout for ways to fill them with interesting flavors and get them to the table faster. This tasty recipe fits the bill nicely, with an authentically flavored spice blend that stirs up in a flash. Refrigerated salsa adds a fresh touch, but jarred salsa still makes a mighty fine taco.

SPICE BLEND

½ teaspoon garlic powder
½ teaspoon onion powder
½ teaspoon oregano, crumbled between the fingers

½ teaspoon chili powder
¼ teaspoon salt
⅛ teaspoon cayenne

FILLING AND TOPPINGS

1 tablespoon vegetable oil
2½ cups shredded rotisserie chicken, pulled apart by hand
3 tablespoons water
8 ready-to-eat regular-size taco shells, warmed according to package directions

Shredded iceberg lettuce or finely-shredded cabbage
Chopped tomatoes
Already-shredded Cheddar cheese or Mexican cheese blend, to taste
Prepared salsa
Light sour cream (optional)

1. **MAKE THE SPICE BLEND:** Stir the ingredients together in a small bowl.

2. **MAKE THE TACOS:** Heat the oil in a 12-inch nonstick skillet over medium heat. Add the chicken and spice blend, and stir to combine. Stir in the water and cook, covered, for 3 minutes, stirring frequently. The chicken should be hot and the spices fragrant. Divide the filling among

the taco shells. Top with the lettuce and tomatoes, and sprinkle with cheese. Spoon on the salsa and sour cream, if using. Serve immediately.

▶ Note

- My family goes back and forth between soft tacos and crispy shells. There is no need to agree. Simply mix and match to suit your taste.

In a Pinch: If you do not have a minute to spare, substitute about 1 tablespoon of your favorite packaged chicken taco seasoning mix for the spice blend.

Serve It Up: Turn your house into a corner Mexican restaurant. Cook up your favorite packaged Spanish rice mix and warm a can of refried beans to round out the plates. I put a bowl of tortilla chips and salsa on the table and we have a little fun with dinner.

ROTISSERIE REUBEN SANDWICH

—Makes 2 sandwiches—

In this recipe a rotisserie chicken pairs with tangy Thousand Island dressing, spunky sauerkraut, and crusty rye bread for a deliciously tasty Reuben without the guilt of the traditional corned beef fare. Satisfying but not heavy, this lighter alternative sports a crispy exterior with a lusciously creamy inside. Serve with pickle spears.

4 slices deli rye bread (about 6¼ × 3½ inches each)

About ⅓ cup Thousand Island dressing, divided

Thinly sliced rotisserie chicken breast to cover 2 slices of bread, skin removed

Pepper, to taste

⅔ cup sauerkraut, preferably jarred, squeezed dry in a paper towel (see Note)

2 slices Swiss cheese (about 1-ounce each)

2 tablespoons butter, divided

1. Spread each slice of bread with the dressing, to taste. Divide the chicken between 2 slices of bread, placing the chicken in a single layer. Sprinkle with pepper, add a thin layer of dressing, and spread the sauerkraut evenly over it. Top with the cheese and the remaining slices of bread, making sure the filling does not spill out the sides. Press the tops down slightly.

2. Melt 1½ tablespoons butter in a 12-inch nonstick skillet over medium heat. Use a spatula to slide the sandwiches into the skillet. Press down on the tops with the spatula and cook until golden brown, about 4 minutes. Turn them over, press the tops down again, and add the remaining ½ tablespoon butter. Cook until the other side is golden and the cheese melts, 3–4 minutes. Turn the sandwiches again, press the tops down again, and cook 1 more minute. Remove to plates, slice in half on the diagonal, and serve.

▶ Notes

- There is a long-standing dispute about the origin of the classic Reuben. Some say it was born in Omaha; others say a New York deli owner first prepared it. No one disputes its delicious appeal.
- If the kids aren't big sauerkraut fans, simply leave it out or replace it with a deli-sliced pickle. It won't be a Reuben but it will still be good.

> **Lighter Touch:** Choose a reduced-fat Thousand Island dressing to lighten this up even further.

QUICK THAI BUNDLES

—Makes 4 servings—

Crisp and refreshing romaine lettuce makes the perfect wrapper for this sandwich. Look for fish sauce in the Asian aisle of the supermarket. You can prepare all the sandwich ingredients ahead of time and then put them together when you are ready to eat. The dressing will keep for a day in the refrigerator.

DRESSING

¼ cup freshly-squeezed lime juice
2 tablespoons peanut butter
1 tablespoon Asian fish sauce (nam pla)
2 teaspoons soy sauce

2 teaspoons jarred chopped ginger
1 teaspoon sugar
Red pepper flakes, to taste (optional)

WRAPS

1½ cups large shreds rotisserie chicken, pulled apart by hand
1 cup bean sprouts (see Note)
1 cup thinly sliced red onion
½ cup already-shredded carrots

½ cup cilantro leaves
⅓ cup chopped roasted peanuts
4 large romaine leaves or rice paper wrappers (see Note)

1. **MAKE THE DRESSING:** Use a fork to whisk the ingredients together in a large bowl.

2. **MAKE THE WRAPS:** Place the chicken, bean sprouts, onions, carrots, cilantro, and peanuts in the bowl with the dressing. Toss well to combine. Place the romaine leaves, curved side up, on a work surface. Spoon about 1 cup of the filling down the middle of each leaf. Serve immediately folding the long sides of the leaves over to eat.

▶ Notes

- When buying bean sprouts, look for whitish ends rather than dark ends, and for sprouts that are crisp when you snap them.
- These sandwiches are great wrapped in rice paper wrappers if you can find them. Look in the Asian section of well-stocked grocery stores or in Asian markets. Rehydrate papers according to package directions. Fill as for the lettuce leaves, fold over, and serve.

POLYNESIAN PIZZA

—Makes 1 pizza (about 11-inches)—

Our sons' love of pineapple pizza prompted me to grab a rotisserie chicken and create this recipe. The sweet-and-sour sauce and the pineapple pieces make this undeniably sweet, but the green onions, chicken, and Canadian bacon prevent it from being cloyingly so. Look for Canadian bacon, a cousin of ham, next to either the bacon or the ham in the self-service deli.

2 cups chopped rotisserie chicken, skin removed

1 bunch green onions, thinly sliced (about 1 cup)

½ cup bottled sweet-and-sour sauce

1 large prebaked pizza crust, regular, not thin

1–2 cups already-shredded Monterey Jack cheese

½ cup chopped Canadian bacon (about 2½-ounces)

1 (8-ounce) can crushed pineapple in juice, drained

1. Position a rack in the center of the oven and preheat the oven to 450° F. Stir the chicken, onions, and sweet-and-sour sauce together in a medium-size bowl. Spread the mixture over the crust, leaving about a ½-inch border. Sprinkle the cheese over all. Top with the Canadian bacon and sprinkle on the pineapple.

2. Bake directly on the rack until the cheese melts and just begins to color, 12–14 minutes. Remove from the oven, cut into wedges, and serve.

▶ Notes

- You can sit and watch while the children assemble the pizza. Your job is to pop it in the oven and cut it after you take it out.
- How much cheese you put on a pizza is largely a matter of preference and how you feel that day. I give a range for the cheese so you can decide how much to sprinkle on.

Company's Coming: Bake a few pizzas and cut them into squares for kids' birthday parties or playdates.

FIESTA PIZZA

—Makes 2 servings—

— 🍴 —

Children and adults alike will love this festive, versatile pizza. The fresh salsa and the chiles dotted on the top are reminiscent of confetti. Easy to prepare, it is a great lunch box or after-school treat for children. Double or triple the recipe for a casual party or video munching and bake them in batches.

2 (8-inch) flour tortillas, soft taco size
½ cup salsa, mild or hot
½ cup finely shredded rotisserie chicken, skin removed and meat pulled apart by hand
½–1 cup already-shredded Mexican blend cheese, or a blend of Cheddar and Monterey Jack cheeses

1 green onion, thinly sliced
2 tablespoons drained mild canned diced chiles
Guacamole, sour cream, or additional salsa (optional)

1. Position a rack in the center of the oven and preheat the oven to 450° F.

2. Place the tortillas on a baking sheet. Spread the salsa over the tortillas, leaving about a ½-inch border on the sides. Top with the chicken and then the cheese. Sprinkle the onion and chiles on top.

3. Bake until the cheese is melted and bubbly, about 6 minutes. The edges will be crispy. Cut into wedges and serve. Top with light dollops of guacamole, sour cream, or additional salsa if desired.

▶ Note
- Stir the salsa before measuring to get a nice mix of juice and salsa pieces.

Lighter Touch: Although they do not melt quite as smoothly as their full-fat cousins, reduced-fat cheeses will work just fine in this recipe.

Company's Coming: This is easy to double or triple and is a great choice when kids or adults drop in unexpectedly. This is also a great late-night snack.

ROASTED PEPPER PIZZA

*_Makes 1 pizza (about 11-inches)_*

It cannot get much easier than this satisfying pizza. The roasted peppers and Italian seasoning add instant and authentic flavor. Buying pizza crusts packed with sauce saves measuring time and eliminates the need to store unused sauce. Or use a generous ½ cup of your own pizza sauce.

1 large, thin prebaked pizza crust with sauce packet

1 cup chopped rotisserie chicken, skin removed

½ teaspoon dried Italian herb seasoning, crumbled between the fingers

1–2 cups already-shredded mozzarella cheese

1 cup sliced mushrooms

½ cup roasted red pepper pieces, sliced into slivers

1. Position a rack in the center of the oven and preheat the oven to 450° F. Spread the sauce on the crust, leaving about a ½-inch border. Top with the chicken. Sprinkle the Italian seasoning, then the cheese over all. Arrange the mushrooms and peppers on the cheese. Bake directly on the rack until the cheese is melted and bubbly, 8–10 minutes. Cut into wedges and serve.

▶ Note

- How much cheese you put on a pizza is largely a matter of preference and how you feel that day. I give a range for the cheese so you can decide how much to sprinkle on.
- Let the kids spread and sprinkle. You just do the baking.

LUNCH BOX PITA POCKET

—Makes 4 sandwiches—

I am always looking for quick, nutritious ways to fill lunch boxes. This easy sandwich fits the bill and is a favorite with kids and adults. Our sons love it because it is colorful, tasty, and loaded with enticing flavors. I love it because of the nutrients from the fruits, veggies, and calcium-rich yogurt. The dressing nicely moistens the pita bread.

DRESSING

1 (8-ounce) container plain yogurt
3 tablespoons mayonnaise
1 tablespoon honey

2–3 teaspoons curry powder
½ teaspoon salt

SANDWICHES

2 cups bite-size chunks rotisserie chicken, skin removed
1 medium tart apple, skin on and chopped into ¼-inch pieces (about 1¼ cups)
½ cup raisins
½ cup already-shredded matchstick-size carrots

2 medium green onions, thinly sliced
4–6 (6-inch) pita rounds
Torn packaged romaine lettuce leaves
2 medium tomatoes, chopped

1. **MAKE THE DRESSING:** Stir the ingredients together in a medium bowl.

2. **MAKE THE SANDWICHES:** Add the chicken, apple, raisins, carrots, and onions to the bowl with the dressing. Stir well to combine. Cut the tops off pita rounds and gently put your fingers inside the bread to open the pockets. Place a little lettuce in each pocket and then divide

the salad among the pockets. Top with a little more lettuce, then the tomatoes. Place on foil and wrap tightly.

▶ Notes

- Select a mild curry powder for children.
- Tomatoes add a sweet juiciness to the sandwich in the first bites so the children do not bite into a mouthful of lettuce.

Lighter Touch: Nonfat yogurt and reduced-fat mayonnaise will lighten this up even more. It will be sweeter and not quite as creamy.

Play It Again: Hollow out a tomato and spoon in any leftover salad for a pretty lunch.

Serve It Up: This is also great served on a bed of lettuce with pita wedges or crackers alongside.

PIZZA-STYLE CROQUE MADAME

—Makes 2 sandwiches—

I use a favorite trick of chefs and blend herbs into butter to boost the flavor of this delectably simple sandwich. Nice and crispy on the outside with a pleasing creamy interior, the roasted red peppers tucked in the middle round out the sandwich and make it a bit more substantial. I like the peppers in water for this, but oil-packed will work fine if that is what you have.

HERB BUTTER

2 tablespoons butter, softened
1 teaspoon dried Italian herb seasoning, crumbled between the fingers

FOR THE SANDWICHES

4 slices sandwich-style white bread
¾–1 cup already-shredded mozzarella or fontina cheese, divided
Thinly sliced rotisserie chicken breast to cover 2 slices of bread, skin removed

2 roasted red peppers packed in water
2 tablespoons softened butter, divided

1. **MAKE THE HERB BUTTER:** Mix the ingredients in a small bowl.

2. **MAKE THE SANDWICHES:** Spread 1 side of each piece of bread with the butter mixture, leaving the pieces buttered side up. Divide ½ of the cheese between 2 slices of bread. Divide the chicken slices evenly between the 2 slices, placing it in a single layer and pressing down firmly. Cut the peppers open so they lay flat and blot them dry with a paper towel. Cover the chicken with a single layer of red peppers, trimming them as needed. Top with the remaining cheese, dividing it evenly between the 2 sandwiches. Cover each sandwich with a second slice of bread, buttered side down. Press down firmly on the sandwich tops.

3. Melt 1 tablespoon of butter in a 12-inch nonstick skillet over medium heat. When the butter sizzles, turn the heat to low. Add the sandwiches and press the tops down with a spatula. Cook until the undersides are golden brown and crispy, 8–10 minutes, pressing the tops down occasionally. Carefully flip the sandwiches over and press the tops down again. Add the remaining tablespoon of butter and cook until the undersides are golden brown and the cheese is melted, about 5 minutes, pressing the tops down occasionally. Let cool for 2–3 minutes, then cut on the diagonal and serve.

▶ Food Fact

- After delving into what really lies between the bread in a Croque Madame, I decided that it depends on where you are and who is preparing the sandwich. Some sources say that in France a fried egg is added to the Croque Monsieur, a toasted ham and cheese sandwich, and in Britain and America the sliced chicken simply nudges out the ham in the Croque Monsieur. Some chefs dip the sandwiches in an egg batter, similar to French toast, before grilling them for what I would call a Monte Cristo. Any way you serve it, they are delicious!

BARBECUE CHICKEN AND COLESLAW BUNS

The best of the barbecue is in the bun with these fun sandwiches. Spice up the slaw a bit if you want a little more bite. Packaged fried onions add just the right crispy crunch. Lemonade, anyone?

2½ cups rotisserie chicken chunks, meat pulled apart by hand

1 cup bottled barbecue sauce, plus more for buns

½ cup thin slices red onion

4 hamburger buns, split in half and lightly toasted

1½ cups deli coleslaw, excess mayonnaise drained

1 cup canned French-fried onions

ACCOMPANIMENTS

Pickles
Potato chips

1. Stir the chicken, barbecue sauce, and onion together in a microwaveable bowl or 4-cup measuring cup. Microwave, covered, on full power for 4 minutes, or until the sauce is bubbly and the chicken is hot. Stir well.

2. Very lightly spread barbecue sauce on the tops of the buns. Spoon the chicken mixture onto the bottom of the buns. Top with the coleslaw and fried onions then the top of the buns. Serve right away with pickles and chips.

TOMATO AND PESTO PIZZA

Makes 1 pizza (about 11-inches)

The pesto and tomatoes make a very pretty and delicious pizza. With ready-to-eat pesto and already-shredded cheese, you can get this delicious, pretty pizza out of the oven in no time.

1 large already-baked pizza crust
1 (6-ounce) container refrigerated pesto
  (about ⅔ cup)
1–1½ cups bite-size chunks rotisserie chicken

1–2 cups already-shredded mozzarella cheese
4 Roma tomatoes, cut into ¼-inch slices

1. Position a rack in the center of the oven and preheat the oven to 450° F. Spread the pesto over the crust, leaving about a ½-inch border. Sprinkle the chicken on the pesto and then sprinkle the cheese over all. Place the tomato slices on top of the cheese. Bake directly on the rack until the cheese is melted and bubbly and the tomatoes have softened, about 15 minutes. Cut into wedges and serve.

▶ Notes
  - How much cheese you put on a pizza is largely a matter of preference and how you feel that day. I give a range for the cheese so you can decide how much to sprinkle on.
  - One cup of chicken is a fine amount. Use 1½ cups if you prefer a lot of chicken flavor.

OLD-FASHIONED CHICKEN SANDWICH

—Makes 1 sandwich—

———— 🍴 ————

Bright, juicy tomato slices and crisp green lettuce peeking out from the golden toast make this American mainstay sandwich as pretty as it is tasty. By all means do not forget it when you have a rotisserie chicken on hand and are looking for something basic and good. Vary the bread and the spreads to suit your tastes.

2 slices lightly toasted sandwich bread, white
    or whole wheat
1½–2 tablespoons mayonnaise, or mustard
    and mayonnaise stirred together
Thinly sliced rotisserie chicken breast to cover
    1 slice of bread

Salt and pepper, to taste
Torn romaine lettuce leaves or iceberg lettuce
Tomato slices

ACCOMPANIMENTS

Fruit or potato chips

1. Lay the bread on a flat work surface and spread to taste with the mayonnaise. Place the chicken on top of 1 slice in a single layer and sprinkle with salt and pepper. Top with the lettuce and tomato. Put the other slice of bread on top, mayonnaise side down, press down lightly, and cut in half. Serve with fruit or potato chips.

VARIATION

Sun-dried Tomato and Chicken Sandwich:
Stir about 2 teaspoons of finely chopped sun-dried tomato and ⅛ teaspoon minced garlic into the mayonnaise.

▶ **Note**

- Keep the bread lightly toasted so that the flavors of the sandwich will come through. If the bread is toasted too dark, the flavor will take over the sandwich.

Lighter Touch: Choose a reduced-fat mayonnaise to lighten this up.

Company's Coming: Make as many as you need and cut in quarters for buffet platters.

KNIFE AND FORK BURRITOS

—Makes 4 servings—

These wet burritos are a great restaurant-style meal-in-a-hurry. I quickly spoon jarred salsa over the burritos before heating them to make these simple burritos just a little different. Put a box of your favorite Spanish rice mix on to cook before you start putting the burritos together. A salad of orange, jicama, and radish slices is good alongside.

SPICE BLEND

⅓ cup light sour cream
1 teaspoon garlic powder
1 teaspoon chili powder

½ teaspoon ground cumin
¼ teaspoon salt

BURRITOS

2½ cups large shreds rotisserie chicken, pulled apart by hand
1 (11-ounce) can Mexican-style corn, drained
2 green onions, sliced (about ¼ cup)
4 burrito-size flour tortillas (about 10-inches across)

1 (16-ounce) can refried beans, beans warmed in microwave
Already-shredded Cheddar cheese, to taste
1 (16-ounce) jar salsa, not chunky

1. **MAKE THE SPICE BLEND:** Stir the ingredients together in a medium bowl.

2. **MAKE THE BURRITOS:** Add the chicken, corn, and onions to the spice blend and stir to combine. Place the tortillas between 2 damp paper towels and microwave until soft, about 20 seconds.

3. Place the tortillas on a work surface and divide the beans among the tortillas. Spread the beans over the tortillas, leaving a 1-inch border around the edges. Spoon the chicken mixture

down the center, sprinkle with cheese, and fold up the bottom 2 inches toward the middle. Fold in the sides 2 inches toward the middle and roll up from the bottom, forming a cylinder.

4. Place the burritos seam side down, on a microwave-safe plate, spoon salsa over the top, and microwave until hot, about 3 minutes. Lift onto plates and serve immediately.

MANGO SPIRALS

—Makes about 4 servings—

I was fascinated by the flavors and textures when I first tasted this style of wrap in San Francisco many years ago. The mix of ingredients ranges from a south-of-the-border wrapper to Indian chutney and truly reflects the global marketplace we eat in today. The mint leaves are quite refreshing and not at all overpowering.

About ⅔ cup whipped cream cheese, at room temperature

2 burrito-size flour tortillas (each about 10-inches across)

½ cup Major Grey's mango chutney, large pieces chopped

1 cup shredded rotisserie chicken, pulled apart by hand

½ large cucumber, peeled and chopped

½ cup mint leaves (optional)

1. Spread the cream cheese over the tortillas, covering them entirely. Spread the chutney over the cream cheese, leaving about a 1-inch border on all sides. Sprinkle the chicken, cucumber, and mint leaves, if using, on top. Roll into tight cylinders, pressing the cream cheese on the edge of the tortillas to seal the wrap. Cut into 2-inch pieces and serve immediately.

THREE-PEPPER HERO

—Makes 4 servings—

The shreds of chicken melt right into the onions and peppers in this enticing sandwich. Hearty but not heavy, you can pair this with your favorite sparkling cider or cold beer for great family game-watching fare.

PEPPER TOPPING

2–3 tablespoons olive oil

1 large red onion, cut in half lengthwise and thinly sliced crosswise (about 2 cups)

1 (16-ounce) bag frozen bell pepper mix (about 2 cups)

2 teaspoons jarred minced garlic

1 teaspoon dried Italian herb seasoning, crumbled between the fingers

½ teaspoon salt, or to taste

SPREAD

½ stick butter (4 tablespoons), softened

3 tablespoons grated Parmesan cheese

1 teaspoon jarred minced garlic

SANDWICHES

4 French-style sandwich rolls (about 6-inches long each), split

2 cups large shreds rotisserie chicken, skin removed and meat pulled apart by hand

2 tablespoons bottled Italian salad dressing

Already-shredded mozzarella cheese, to taste

1. Position a rack in the center of the oven and preheat the oven to 450° F.

2. **MAKE THE PEPPER TOPPING:** Heat the oil in a 12-inch nonstick skillet over medium-high heat. Add the onion and peppers, and cook, stirring frequently, just until the onion softens, and the peppers are tender, about 8 minutes. Add the garlic, Italian seasoning, and salt, and cook for 2 minutes, stirring constantly.

3. **MAKE THE SPREAD:** While the peppers are cooking, stir the ingredients together in a small bowl.

4. **MAKE THE SANDWICHES:** Coat each piece of bread with the spread and place, spread side up, on a baking sheet. Divide the chicken among the bottoms of the rolls, drizzle with the salad dressing, and spread on the pepper topping. Sprinkle cheese on top. Bake until the cheese melts, about 5 minutes. Cover immediately with the hot roll tops and press down. Slice on the diagonal and serve.

Lighter Touch: These are great open-faced. Just start with two rolls instead of four, use a light salad dressing, and go light on the cheese.

Company's Coming: Make this on a long French roll and cut it into smaller pieces for a great centerpiece for a casual get-together.

Do-Ahead Tip: You can prepare the spread and peppers a day in advance. Let the spread come to room temperature before using, and warm the peppers gently in the microwave or a skillet just to take the chill off.

Serve It Up: Serve bowls of steaming hot soup alongside for a cozy dinner.

CLASSIC CHICKEN QUESADILLA

—Makes 1 serving—

Quesadillas are the Mexican equivalent of American grilled cheese sandwiches. I like to warm the tortilla and flip it over before sprinkling the cheese because I find that the cheese melts better.

1 burrito-size flour tortilla (about 10 inches across)

About ¾ cup already-shredded Mexican blend cheese

½ cup finely chopped rotisserie chicken, skin removed

1–2 green onions, thinly sliced

ACCOMPANIMENTS

Salsa
Sour cream
Prepared guacamole

1. Heat a 12-inch nonstick skillet over medium-high heat. Put the tortilla in the pan and heat until the underside is warm but has not browned, about 1 minute. Flip the tortilla over with a spatula and sprinkle cheese over the entire tortilla, leaving about a ¼-inch border. Sprinkle the chicken and onion over half of the tortilla. Fold the other half over the chicken with the spatula, press down slightly, and heat until the underside is a light brown, about 2 minutes. Press down occasionally. Flip it over with the spatula and heat until the other side is light brown, about 1 minute, pressing down frequently.

2. Slide the quesadilla onto a work surface, cut in quarters, and serve with the desired accompaniments.

▶ Note

- If you want to make more quesadillas at one time, bake them in the oven. Preheat the oven to 400° F. Place as many tortillas as desired on a baking sheet. Sprinkle with cheese, sliced onion, chicken, and a little more cheese. Top with another tortilla, press down firmly, and bake until golden brown on top, about 5 minutes. The edges may crisp a little. Cut into wedges and serve.

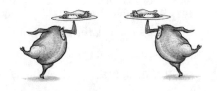

COZY CASSEROLES

Casseroles are one of life's culinary lifesavers. Typically quick to put together and welcome by all, these homey dishes make their way to the table for occasions ranging from potlucks to an intimate dinner with friends. I never tire of coming up with new all-in-one dishes to serve because the convenience and flavor possibilities fit so well with the way we eat. I can add a vegetable here, an interesting sauce there, and, of course, my trusty rotisserie chicken, and in no time flat I have what I call a "taste good, feel good" meal.

People often think of casseroles as being baked in the oven, but a casserole doesn't have to be baked. Whenever I stir everything into one dish, serve it from the same pot or pan, and come up with that casserole feeling, I call it a casserole. Other dishes in this book may also be all in one, but the selections in this chapter are the simple, unassuming, tasty fare that easily fits the "serve yourself" status of casserole.

With recipes ranging from Homestyle Chicken Noodle Casserole to Topsy-Turvy Tamale Pie, these dishes are good, and there's no gloppy cafeteria fare in sight. Once you try these, you will never again be reluctant to sign up for a casserole when the potluck sheet comes around. You will be first in line with a casserole using your secret weapon—a rotisserie chicken.

LICKETY-SPLIT LASAGNA

—Makes about 8 servings—

No need to reach for frozen lasagna when a rotisserie chicken and no-boil noodles can get delicious homemade lasagna to your table so quickly. This recipe looks long, but it is as easy as it can be. This makes a good-size pan and reheats well, making it great for potlucks and for quick lunches later in the week.

RICOTTA FILLING

- 1 large egg
- 1 (15-ounce) container ricotta cheese (about 1¾ cups)
- 1 (10-ounce) box frozen chopped spinach, thawed and squeezed dry
- 1 teaspoon dried Italian herb seasoning, crumbled between the fingers
- ¼ teaspoon ground nutmeg
- 3 cups already-shredded mozzarella cheese, divided
- ⅔ cup already-shredded Parmesan cheese, divided

CHICKEN FILLING

- 2½ cups large shreds rotisserie chicken, pulled apart by hand
- 1 (26 to 28-ounce) jar spaghetti sauce
- 1 (6-ounce) package sliced mushrooms (about 2 cups)
- 1 (8-ounce) can Italian-seasoned tomato sauce (1 cup)
- 1 tablespoon jarred minced garlic

9 no-boil, oven-ready lasagna noodles

1. Place a rack in the center of the oven and preheat the oven to 400° F. Use nonstick cooking spray to lightly coat a 13 × 9-inch pan and a piece of foil large enough to cover the pan.

2. **MAKE THE RICOTTA FILLING:** Lightly beat the egg in a medium bowl. Stir in the ricotta, spinach, Italian seasoning, and nutmeg. Stir in 2 cups mozzarella cheese and ⅓ cup Parmesan cheese.

3. **MAKE THE CHICKEN FILLING:** Stir the chicken, spaghetti sauce, mushrooms, tomato sauce, and garlic together in a large bowl.

4. **ASSEMBLE THE LASAGNA:** Spread about 1½ cups of the chicken filling in the bottom of the pan. Place 3 lasagna noodles crosswise over the filling, leaving space between the noodles and between the noodles and the side of the pan. Spread a generous 1½ cups of the ricotta filling over the pasta. Repeat the chicken filling, lasagna noodles, and ricotta filling layers 2 more times. Top with a layer of chicken filling. Combine the remaining 1 cup of mozzarella cheese and ⅓ cup Parmesan cheese. Sprinkle over the top and press down lightly. Cover loosely with foil and bake for 45 minutes. Remove the foil and bake until bubbly, about 15 minutes. Let rest for 5 to 10 minutes before serving.

▶ Note

- The noodles may or may not touch in the finished dish. Don't worry if there are small gaps; it will be every bit as delicious.

Lighter Touch: Choose part-skim ricotta.

Play It Again: This keeps well in the fridge for a day or two. Reheat in the microwave. Freeze for longer storage.

Company's Coming: This is the perfect lasagna for entertaining—delicious and so easy that you will be rested enough to enjoy your guests. It can also be baked a day ahead and reheated.

SCALLOPED POTATOES AND GREEN BEANS

—Makes 4–6 servings—

Canned potatoes, a quick microwave sauce, and my trusty rotisserie chicken get this good and simple meal to the table in no time flat. The addition of green beans makes this a whole meal since it has chicken, a starch, and a green vegetable. Remember this for every day and holidays.

SPICE BLEND

½ teaspoon garlic powder
½ teaspoon onion powder

½ teaspoon salt
¼ teaspoon pepper

SAUCE

1½ cups milk
1 tablespoon butter
2 tablespoons cornstarch mixed with
    ¼ cup cold milk

2 cups already-shredded sharp Cheddar
    cheese (8 ounces), divided
1 tablespoon Dijon mustard

POTATO MIXTURE

2 (14½-ounce each) cans sliced new potatoes,
    drained
1½ cups bite-size chunks rotisserie chicken

1 cup frozen whole petite green beans
1 (2-ounce) jar sliced pimentos, drained
    (¼ cup)

1. Position a rack in the bottom third of the oven and preheat the oven to 375° F. Lightly coat a shallow 2-quart baking dish with nonstick cooking spray.

2. **MAKE THE SPICE BLEND:** Stir the ingredients together in a small bowl and set aside.

3. **MAKE THE SAUCE:** Place the milk and butter in a large microwaveable bowl. Microwave on high power, covered, until boiling, 4–5 minutes. Stir the cornstarch mixture then stir it into the bowl until thoroughly combined. Stir in the spice blend, 1½ cups of the cheese, and the mustard. Stir in the ingredients for the potato mixture.

4. Pour the contents of the bowl into the prepared pan and sprinkle with the remaining ½ cup of cheese. Bake until bubbly, about 30 minutes. Let rest for 5–10 minutes before serving to let the potatoes absorb the liquid.

▶ Note
- I use my trusty old 9¼ × 9¼-inch glass baking dish for this. My recipe tester used an 8 × 8-inch glass baking dish that worked just fine. If you are not sure how many quarts your dish holds, use a measuring cup to fill the dish with water and count how many cups it takes to fill the dish.

Measuring Tip: Cornstarch clumps. To measure, dip the spoon into the box and level it off with a knife. Break up the clumps before adding the milk.

Lighter Touch: Use 2% milk and reduced-fat cheese.

EVERYDAY ENCHILADA CASSEROLE

—Makes 6 servings—

———— ❦ ————

This is a fine choice when you want a quick, simple casserole with a Mexican flair. Serve refried beans, packaged Spanish rice, and orange slices alongside.

FILLING

2½–3 cups shredded rotisserie chicken, pulled apart by hand

½ large onion, chopped (about ½ cup)

½ cup already-shredded Mexican blend cheese, plus more for top

1 (4-ounce) can mild diced green chiles, drained

2 tablespoons chopped cilantro

2 tablespoons jarred minced garlic

1 teaspoon cumin seed

½ teaspoon salt

12 corn tortillas (5½ to 6-inches across, not super-size)

1 (24-ounce) jar chunky salsa

1. Position a rack in the bottom third of the oven and preheat the oven to 350° F. Use nonstick cooking spray to lightly coat a 13 × 9-inch pan and a piece of foil large enough to cover the pan. Set aside.

2. **MAKE THE FILLING:** Stir the filling ingredients together in a medium bowl, adding the ½ cup of cheese.

3. Microwave a stack of 6 tortillas between damp paper towels on high power until the tortillas are hot and soft enough to roll, about 1 minute. Cover with a cloth towel to keep warm. Remove 1 tortilla at a time, keeping the other tortillas covered, and place a rounded ⅓ cup of filling

down the center. Roll into a cylinder and place, seam side down, in the prepared pan. Repeat with the remaining tortillas, placing them close enough to touch. Microwave and fill the remaining 6 tortillas.

4. Cover the pan with the prepared foil and bake for 15 minutes. Remove the foil, spread the salsa over the top, and sprinkle with cheese, as desired. Bake loosely covered, until the enchiladas are hot and the sauce is bubbly, about 20 minutes.

Company's Coming: This is a great meal for unexpected guests.

BROCCOLI AND CROUTON STRATA

—Makes 6–8 servings—

Stratas are bread puddings that typically soak overnight before baking. The convenience of good-quality packaged croutons and frozen broccoli in cheese sauce lets me quickly serve a strata for an everyday meal. This one has a good combination of flavors with a little punch from the ham. Serve tomato slices alongside.

SPICE BLEND

1 teaspoon paprika
¼ teaspoon ground nutmeg

¼ teaspoon salt
Pinch of cayenne

FILLING

6 large eggs
1 (12-ounce) can evaporated milk
½ cup milk
2 (10-ounce) packages frozen broccoli with cheese sauce, defrosted in microwave and stirred

1½ cups bite-size chunks rotisserie chicken
⅔ cup bite-size chunks deli ham
½ cup finely chopped red onion
1 (5-ounce) box garlic and butter French bread croutons (about 4 cups)
1 cup already-shredded sharp Cheddar cheese

1. Position a rack in the center of the oven and preheat the oven to 325° F. Lightly coat a 13 × 9-inch pan with nonstick cooking spray.

2. **MAKE THE SPICE BLEND:** Stir the ingredients together in a large bowl.

3. **MAKE THE FILLING:** Add the eggs to the bowl with the spice blend and beat together to break up the eggs. Add the evaporated milk and milk, and stir until thoroughly combined. Stir

in the broccoli and cheese sauce, chicken, ham, and onion, stirring well to combine. Add the croutons and mix well to moisten, then stir in the cheese. Spoon into the prepared pan, press the croutons down with the back of a wooden spoon, and let the pan sit for 15 minutes to help the croutons absorb the liquid.

4. Bake for 20 minutes, then press the top down firmly with the back of a wooden spoon. Continue baking until bubbly and the middle moves just slightly when you jiggle the pan, about 30–35 minutes longer. Let rest for 15 minutes before cutting.

▶ **Notes**
- Stirring is everything with this quick treat of a meal since everything should be combined well in order for it to bake as evenly as possible. It takes only a few minutes to do it right, so don't skimp on the effort.
- This is one of my favorite dishes to put together with my sons because it is a forgiving dump-and-stir with no fussy ingredients. Just use a big bowl and don't worry about the splashes.

Play It Again: This heats up well the next day.

Company's Coming: Perfect for guests, and if you keep everything else simple, even the kids will love it.

Lighter Touch: Use nonfat evaporated milk, 2% milk, and reduced fat cheese.

ORANGE AND CREAM CHEESE CHICKEN CRÊPES

—Makes 4 servings—

My recipe tester, Maria, and I put our heads and tummies together to develop this delightful, almost dessert-like recipe. We agreed that it makes a great light dinner or a stupendous brunch or shower dish. Look for the crêpes in the produce section of your supermarket.

⅓ cup frozen orange juice concentrate, thawed

2 tablespoons butter

2 tablespoons orange marmalade

1 (8-ounce) container whipped cream cheese

2 cups shredded rotisserie chicken, skin removed and meat pulled apart by hand

½ cup dried cranberries

¼ cup slivered almonds

4 ready-to-eat crêpes

1. Position a rack in the bottom third of the oven and preheat the oven to 400° F. Lightly coat an 8 × 8-inch baking pan with nonstick cooking spray. Set aside.

2. Combine the orange juice concentrate, butter, and marmalade in a medium saucepan. Warm just until the butter and marmalade melt, stirring frequently. Remove ⅓ cup of sauce and set aside.

3. Stir the cream cheese into the sauce in the saucepan, stirring until smooth. Stir in the chicken, cranberries, and almonds.

4. Spoon about ¾ cup of filling down the center of each crêpe. Roll into cylinders and place, seam side down, in the baking dish. Cover with foil and bake until heated through, about 15 minutes. Drizzle with the remaining sauce and serve immediately.

Just You or Two: These make quite a lovely candlelight dinner. Sprinkle a few dried cranberries over the sauce for color.

Company's Coming: Double this recipe for a great brunch. Make the filling a day ahead and let it come to room temperature before filling the crêpes. Bake in a 13×9-inch pan.

NACHO DINNER BAKE

—Makes 6–8 servings—

Nachos for dinner? You bet—with this super-quick meal in one that takes nachos far beyond munch and crunch and includes foods from all over the food pyramid. Inspired by a recipe I saw in a magazine, this stir-and-bake dish is a great way to get the whole family involved in putting together a quick dinner. Older children can show off their maturity by cutting the chicken and onions and by watching the oven. Young children are always eager to stir and spread, and will happily put the chips in the pan.

FILLING

About 12 cups tortilla chips (about ⅔ of
   a 14-ounce bag)
2 cups chopped rotisserie chicken
1 (11-ounce) can Mexican-style corn with red
   and green peppers, drained
½ bunch sliced green onions (about ½ cup)

½ cup light sour cream
1 tablespoon chili powder
1 teaspoon ground cumin
½ teaspoon garlic powder
½ teaspoon salt

TOPPING

1 (15-ounce) can black beans, drained and rinsed
1 (16-ounce) jar salsa
Already-shredded Mexican blend cheese, to taste

GARNISH

Avocado slices
Light sour cream

1. Position a rack in the bottom third of the oven and preheat the oven to 450° F. Lightly coat a glass 13 × 9-inch pan with nonstick cooking spray.

2. **MAKE THE FILLING:** Line the bottom and sides of the pan with chips. Stir the remaining filling ingredients together in a medium bowl and spoon the mixture into the pan.

3. **ASSEMBLE THE TOPPING:** Sprinkle the beans over the filling and then spread the salsa over the beans. Sprinkle cheese, as desired, over all. Bake until the filling is hot and the cheese is melted, about 15 minutes. Serve immediately, scooping it out with a serving spoon. Garnish as desired.

▶ Note

- Try different types of chips and salsa. Black bean chips give a deeper flavor, while chipotle salsa gives a dish more bite.

In a Pinch: In a bigger hurry? Stir 4 teaspoons of your favorite chicken taco mix into the filling instead of the chili powder, cumin, garlic powder, and salt.

Lighter Touch: Choose baked chips and use a reduced-fat Cheddar cheese.

CHICKEN AND BISCUIT POT PIE

—Makes 4-6 servings—

Chicken pot pie is certain to be high on the list of America's favorite comfort foods. This version is topped with biscuits and baked right in the skillet to let you dig in in a hurry. Use a large nonmetal spoon to serve right from the skillet, scooping up the golden biscuits and the filling underneath. The filling will run when you scoop since the pie is not baked in individual serving sizes.

FILLING

2 tablespoons butter
1 large onion, chopped (about 1 cup)
1 cup already-sliced mushrooms
1 large rib celery, sliced crosswise into
 ⅛-inch pieces
2½ cups bite-size chunks rotisserie chicken,
 white and dark meat

1 (14½-ounce) can fat-free less-sodium
 chicken broth (about 1¾ cups)
1 (10¾-ounce) can condensed cream of
 potato soup, undiluted
1 cup frozen peas and carrots
1 teaspoon poultry seasoning
⅛ teaspoon pepper

TOPPING

1 (16.3-ounce) tube large-size flaky layer refrigerated buttermilk biscuits
2 tablespoons milk
½ teaspoon dried thyme, crumbled between the fingers

1. **MAKE THE FILLING:** Position a rack in the center of the oven and preheat the oven to 350° F. Melt the butter in a 12-inch nonstick skillet over medium-high heat. Add the onion, mushrooms, and celery, and cook, stirring frequently, until the mushrooms begin to lose their juices and the celery begins to soften, about 4 minutes. Lower the heat to medium and stir in

the chicken, broth, soup, peas and carrots, poultry seasoning, and pepper. Bring to a simmer and cook for 4 minutes, stirring frequently.

2. **ASSEMBLE THE TOPPING:** Wrap the skillet handle in foil if it is not ovenproof. Divide the biscuits into 12 equal pieces and place them over the filling, putting them close enough for the sides of the biscuits to touch. Brush the tops of the biscuits with milk and sprinkle with the thyme. Bake until the tops of the biscuits are golden brown, about 20 minutes. Serve immediately.

Lighter Touch: Select reduced-fat biscuits.

In a Pinch: If time is truly short, serve chicken and biscuits. Bake the biscuits according to package directions and make the filling while the biscuits bake, simmering the filling for 10 minutes. Split the hot biscuits in half and spoon the filling over the top.

Company's Coming: Spoon the filling into individual ovenproof soup tureens, top with a biscuit, and bake.

TOPSY-TURVY TAMALE PIE

—Makes 4–6 servings—

What a treat! You can have the comfort of a homemade tamale pie without cooking cornmeal and laboring over the filling. I punch up store-bought corn muffin mix with chiles and spices for topping flavor in a zip and use a rotisserie chicken to create a quick, tasty filling. It takes quite a few ingredients but very little time to get this robust skillet tamale pie to the table.

SPICE BLEND

2 tablespoons chili powder
1 teaspoon dried oregano, crumbled between the fingers
1 teaspoon cumin seeds
½ teaspoon salt

FILLING

1 tablespoon vegetable oil
1 large onion, chopped (about 1 cup)
1 cup firmly packed frozen pepper strips (about one-third of a 14-ounce bag), chopped
1 teaspoon jarred minced garlic
2 (10-ounce) cans diced tomatoes with chiles
2½ cups large chunks rotisserie chicken
1 (15-ounce) can pinto beans, drained and rinsed
1 cup frozen corn kernels or 1 (7-ounce) can of corn, drained
1 (3.8-ounce) can sliced black ripe olives, drained (about 1 cup)

TOPPING

1 (8½-ounce) box corn muffin mix (about 1½ cups mix, enough for 6–10 muffins)

1 cup already-shredded sharp Cheddar cheese, divided

1 (4-ounce) can diced mild chile peppers, undrained

⅓ cup milk

1 egg

1 teaspoon chili powder

1. Preheat the oven to 350° F.

2. **MAKE THE SPICE BLEND:** Stir the ingredients together in a small bowl and set aside.

3. **MAKE THE FILLING:** Heat the oil in a 12-inch nonstick skillet over medium heat. Add the onion and bell peppers, and cook, stirring frequently, until the onion begins to soften, about 4 minutes. Add the garlic and spice blend, and cook 2 more minutes, stirring constantly. Add the tomatoes, chicken, beans, corn, and olives. Stir well to combine and bring to a simmer. Turn the heat to low and let the mixture simmer while you make the topping, stirring occasionally. Wrap the skillet handle in foil if it is not ovenproof.

4. **MAKE THE TOPPING:** Mix the ingredients together in a small bowl, stirring in ½ cup cheese. Spoon the topping over the skillet, leaving a ½-inch border. Sprinkle with the remaining ½ cup cheese. Bake for 15–20 minutes, until the top is firm but springy when touched lightly, or until a knife inserted in the center of the topping comes out clean. Serve immediately.

Lighter Touch: Use reduced-fat cheese.

good

HOMESTYLE CHICKEN NOODLE CASSEROLE

—Makes 4–6 servings—

This is my rotisserie chicken version of a long-standing best-seller at one of our local grocery stores. Shoppers gobble this up day after day, year after year, store after store. Your family will, too.

NOODLES

3 quarts water
1 teaspoon salt
4 cups wide dry egg noodles (about 6 ounces)

SPICE BLEND

1 teaspoon garlic powder
1 teaspoon onion powder
½ teaspoon paprika

½ teaspoon salt
½ teaspoon pepper

CASSEROLE

1 tablespoon butter
1 large rib celery, sliced into ¼-inch pieces (about ⅔ cup)
1 (10¾-ounce) can condensed cream of celery soup, undiluted

1 cup milk
2 cups bite-size chunks rotisserie chicken
1 cup frozen peas and carrots
1 (8-ounce) container light sour cream (about 1 cup)

1. **MAKE THE NOODLES:** Bring the water and salt to a boil in a large pot. Add the noodles and cook according to package directions until just tender. Drain and rinse in hot water. Shake off the excess water and return the noodles to the pot. Cover to keep warm.

2. **MAKE THE SPICE BLEND:** Meanwhile, stir the ingredients together in a small bowl and set aside.

3. **MAKE THE CASSEROLE:** Melt the butter in a 3-quart saucepan over medium heat. Add the celery and cook, stirring frequently, until it begins to soften, about 4 minutes. Add the soup, milk, and spice blend. Stir well and bring to a boil, stirring frequently. Add the chicken and peas and carrots, and stir well. Bring to a simmer, turn the heat to low, and simmer, covered, for 10 minutes, stirring occasionally. Stir in the sour cream and noodles. Heat through, about 3 minutes, stirring frequently. Do not boil. Serve immediately.

> **Lighter Touch:** Use the reduced fat variety of soup and 1% milk.

CREAMY CORN AND SPINACH ENCHILADAS

—Makes 12 enchiladas—

These enchiladas have a creamy richness that is hard to resist. They also have a nice tang from the tomatillo-based green sauce. Scrumptious and fast, the creamed spinach and cream-style corn tucked inside make them even more luscious. Serve with sliced tomatoes and just wait for the "mmm's."

FILLING

2 tablespoons vegetable oil

1 large onion, chopped (about 1 cup)

2½ cups shredded rotisserie chicken, pulled apart by hand

1 (4-ounce) can diced mild green chiles

2 teaspoons chili powder

1 (14¾-ounce) can cream-style corn

1 (10-ounce) box frozen creamed spinach, thawed

½ cup light sour cream

1 cup already-shredded Monterey Jack cheese (4-ounces)

½ teaspoon salt

12 super size corn tortillas (each about 6½-inches across)

SAUCE

¾ cup green taco sauce or salsa verde, not chunky

½ cup light sour cream

Already-shredded Monterey Jack cheese, to taste

½ cup finely chopped cilantro

1. Position a rack in the bottom third of the oven and preheat the oven to 350° F. Lightly coat a 13 × 9-inch pan and a piece of foil large enough to cover the pan with nonstick cooking spray.

2. **MAKE THE FILLING:** Heat the oil in a 12-inch nonstick skillet over medium-high heat. Add the onion and cook, stirring frequently, until it is clear, about 4 minutes. Add the chicken, chiles, and chili powder, and cook for 2 minutes, stirring constantly. Remove from the heat and stir in the corn, spinach, sour cream, cheese, and salt.

3. Place a stack of 6 tortillas between damp paper towels and microwave on high power until the tortillas are hot and soft enough to roll, about 1 minute. Cover with a cloth towel to keep warm. Remove 1 tortilla at a time, keeping the other tortillas covered, and place a rounded ⅓ cup of the filling down the center. Roll into a cylinder and place in the prepared pan, seam side down and close enough to touch. Repeat with the remaining tortillas. Microwave and fill the remaining 6 tortillas. Cover the pan tightly with foil and bake until the enchiladas are hot, about 30 minutes.

4. **MAKE THE SAUCE:** Meanwhile, stir the taco sauce and sour cream together in a small bowl. Uncover the pan and spread the sauce over the hot enchiladas. Sprinkle cheese and cilantro over the top. Return to the oven, uncovered, and bake until the cheese melts and the sauce is bubbly, about 10 minutes.

▶ Note

- Use a metal measuring cup to scoop the filling. This will keep the sizes approximately the same for even baking.

Lighter Touch: Microwaving the tortillas instead of frying already makes these lighter than the traditional enchiladas. You can reduce the fat a little more by using a reduced-fat cheese and creamed spinach in a low-fat sauce. However, I do not suggest a fat-free sour cream. Each enchilada has only a little more than 1 tablespoon of light sour cream, which is probably fine for all but the strictest of diets.

Serve It Up: These are great for parties and buffets.

PASTA CORDON BLEU

—Makes 4–6 servings—

———— ✦ ————

This rich and creamy pasta version of chicken cordon bleu—the ham and cheese–stuffed chicken breast—is sure to be a favorite with your family. Ask the deli to cut a thick piece of ham for you and then chop it when you get home. The bread crumbs add an appealing crunch that kids love, but if you are pressed for time, you can skip that step and simmer the dish on the stovetop for 10–15 minutes. The ½ teaspoon of pepper is not an error; it is just right.

SPICE BLEND

1 teaspoon dried thyme, crumbled between the fingers
½ teaspoon pepper
¼ teaspoon salt

PASTA

2 cups large elbow macaroni, cooked until firm with ½ teaspoon salt according to package directions and rinsed in hot water
2 tablespoons butter
1 large onion, chopped (about 1 cup)
2 teaspoons jarred minced garlic
2 cups milk
1 (10¾-ounce) can condensed cream of chicken soup, undiluted

3 tablespoons Dijon mustard
2 cups bite-size chunks rotisserie chicken
2 cups shredded Swiss cheese
1½ cups frozen peas
1 cup bite-size chunks deli ham (about 6 ounces)
⅓ cup Italian-style dry bread crumbs

1. Position a rack in the center of the oven and preheat the oven to 350° F.

2. **MAKE THE SPICE BLEND:** Stir the ingredients together in a small bowl and set aside.

3. **MAKE THE PASTA:** Shake any excess water off the pasta and set the pasta aside. Melt the butter in a 12-inch nonstick skillet over medium heat. Add the onion and cook, stirring frequently, until it begins to soften, about 4 minutes. Add the garlic, sprinkle with the spice blend, and cook for 1 minute, stirring constantly. Stir in the milk, soup, and mustard, and bring to a boil. Stir frequently. Add the pasta, chicken, cheese, peas, and ham, and stir well. Bring to a simmer and cook about 3 minutes, stirring occasionally.

4. Remove from the heat and sprinkle the bread crumbs evenly over the top. Wrap the skillet handle in foil if it is not ovenproof. Bake until the pasta is bubbly and the bread crumbs begin to brown, about 25 minutes. Serve immediately.

Lighter Touch: Choose a reduced-fat ham, the reduced-fat less-sodium variety of the soup, and 2% milk.

Play It Again: This dish reheats well.

Company's Coming: Spoon the hot mixture into a buttered baking dish, sprinkle with the bread crumbs, and then set the table while your dinner bubbles away in the oven.

STUFFING IN A SKILLET

—Makes 4–6 servings—

You can enjoy the stuffing and the chicken all in the same hearty dish with this quick and easy family dinner. Choose button or cremini mushrooms, or a wild mushroom blend, depending on your mood and your pocketbook.

SPICE BLEND

1 teaspoon paprika

½ teaspoon dried thyme, crumbled between the fingers

¼ teaspoon dried rosemary, crumbled between the fingers

¼ teaspoon pepper

STUFFING

2½ cups milk

3 tablespoons butter

1 medium onion, chopped (about ¾ cup)

1 large rib celery, sliced

1 (6-ounce) package sliced mushrooms (about 2 cups)

1 teaspoon jarred minced garlic

1 (6-ounce) package chicken-flavored dried stuffing mix (about 2¾ cups)

2 cups bite-size chunks rotisserie chicken

1 (10¾-ounce) can condensed cream of chicken soup, undiluted

⅔ cup dried cranberries or raisins

1. Preheat the oven to 350° F.

2. **MAKE THE SPICE BLEND:** Stir the ingredients together in a small bowl and set aside.

3. **MAKE THE STUFFING:** Microwave the milk in a 4-cup measure until very hot. Set aside. Melt the butter in a 12-inch nonstick skillet over medium heat. Add the onion and celery, and cook, stirring frequently, until they begin to soften, about 5 minutes. Add the mushrooms and

garlic, sprinkle with the spice blend, and cook, stirring frequently, until the mushrooms lose their liquid and just begin to brown, about 4 minutes. Sprinkle the stuffing mix over the pan, add the hot milk, and stir well. Add the soup, and cranberries, and stir well to combine. Cook, stirring frequently, until the stuffing absorbs the liquid, about 3 minutes. Wrap the skillet handle in foil if it is not ovenproof. Bake until the top is just firm, about 20 minutes.

VARIATION

Spinach Stuffing:

Add ½ teaspoon grated nutmeg to the spice blend. Thaw one 10-ounce package of chopped spinach and squeeze dry. Stir the spinach in along with the chicken, soup, and cranberries. Stir in ¼ cup grated Parmesan cheese and proceed with the recipe.

Lighter Touch: Try the reduced-fat less-sodium variety of soup and 1% milk.

DINNER IN A POT OR A PAN

Bursting with flavor, texture, and bright colors, the recipes in this chapter are fresh and exciting. They reflect the way we eat today—with vegetables sneaking into many bites and sauces trading complexity of flavor for simple heaviness. With these recipes in hand, rotisserie chickens can play the lead in anything from Quick Coq au Vin to Hurry Curry. These dishes offer variety and a wide range of flavors. Sometimes the recipes call for removing the meat from the bone; other times the whole chicken is cut into serving pieces. Either way, the dishes are delicious and the recipes are new traditions in the making.

CHICKEN À L'ORANGE

—Makes 4 servings—

This rotisserie chicken version of the duck classic is a family-pleasing meal that you can have on the table in no time flat. I remove the skin since it holds most of the spices in rotisserie chickens, and I like the orange sauce to come right through. Serve with packaged rice pilaf with slivered almonds and green beans for a delightful and pretty dinner.

SPICE BLEND

½ teaspoon ground ginger
½ teaspoon dry mustard

½ teaspoon salt
½ teaspoon white pepper

SAUCE

1 cup frozen orange juice concentrate, thawed
2 tablespoons orange marmalade
2 tablespoons butter
½ cup water

1 tablespoon cornstarch mixed with
    2 tablespoons cold water
2 teaspoons freshly-squeezed lemon juice

CHICKEN

2 medium seedless oranges, sliced into ¼-inch rounds
1 rotisserie chicken, cut into serving pieces and skin removed

1. Preheat the oven to 400° F. Lightly coat a 13 × 9-inch pan with nonstick cooking spray. Set aside.

2. **MAKE THE SPICE BLEND:** Stir the ingredients together in a 2-quart saucepan.

3. **MAKE THE SAUCE:** Add the orange juice concentrate, marmalade, butter, and water to the saucepan with the spice blend, stirring well. Bring to a boil over medium heat and cook, stirring frequently, until the mixture begins to thicken, about 5 minutes. Stir the cornstarch and water mixture, then stir it into the sauce. Boil 2 more minutes, stirring frequently. Remove from the heat and stir in the lemon juice.

4. **MAKE THE CHICKEN:** Place the orange slices in a single layer in the prepared pan and arrange the chicken pieces on top, leaving space between the pieces. Spoon the sauce over the chicken and bake until the sauce is bubbly and the chicken is heated through, about 20 minutes. Serve immediately, spooning the oranges and sauce over the chicken.

▶ Note

- Thaw the can of orange juice quickly by placing the unopened can in a bowl of hot water.

Company's Coming: A wonderful and quick company dish with a special touch.

CHICKEN HASH

—Makes 2–3 servings—

A rotisserie chicken lets me enjoy a version of one of my favorite Thanksgiving leftovers, a gravy-rich hash, as often as I please. There are as many styles of hash as there are cooks, ranging from the dried "corned beef hash" style to the wetter varieties. This is my dad's version. It has a nice and creamy texture and is terrific when there are just a few of you and you want dinner in a hurry. Serve with a green salad.

3 tablespoons butter
1 large onion, chopped (about 1 cup)
1 medium red bell pepper, chopped (about ¾ cup)
2 teaspoons jarred minced garlic
2 teaspoons paprika
⅓ cup all-purpose flour
1 (14½-ounce) can fat-free less-sodium chicken broth (about 1¾ cups)

2½ cups bite-size chunks rotisserie chicken
2 cups chopped cooked red potatoes, unpeeled
½ teaspoon salt
⅓ cup heavy (whipping) cream
¼ cup chopped flat-leaf (Italian) parsley
Pepper, to taste

1. Melt the butter in a 12-inch nonstick skillet over medium-high heat. Add the onion and bell pepper, and cook, stirring frequently, until the onion is clear and the pepper is crisp-tender, about 3 minutes. Lower the heat to medium, add the garlic and paprika, and cook for 1 minute, stirring constantly.

2. Sprinkle the flour over the vegetables and cook, stirring constantly, until the flour turns a golden brown, about 2 minutes. Stir in the broth a little at a time, stirring constantly and breaking up any lumps. The mixture should be smooth. Bring to a boil and then add the chicken, potatoes, and salt, and stir. Turn the heat to low, stir in the cream, and simmer about 5 minutes to heat through, stirring frequently. Do not boil. Stir in the parsley and pepper.

▶ **Note**

- If you do not have cooked potatoes, look for chopped, cooked potatoes in the freezer case. You can also look for raw chopped potatoes in the produce section, or cut raw potatoes into pieces. Microwave quickly or boil them just until fork tender.

Produce Pick: Flat-leaf parsley has a milder flavor than its curly cousin. I use it here so that the parsley flavor does not overpower the dish.

Breakfast Pick: I like this for breakfast served with toast and a tall glass of orange juice.

HURRY CURRY

—Makes 4 servings—

There is nothing fancy about this deliciously satisfying curry. Served over steamed rice, it is just plain good and goes together in a snap without sacrificing flavor. Select a mild curry powder for a dish that children and adults will love, or choose a hotter powder if everyone is a spice lover. Dinner is served in no time if you start your favorite rice before you start making the curry.

2 tablespoons vegetable oil

1½ cups chopped onion (about 2 medium onions)

1½ cups baby carrots, sliced into ¼-inch rounds (about 5 ounces)

2 tablespoons curry powder

1 teaspoon jarred minced garlic

¼ cup all-purpose flour

2 (14½-ounce) cans fat-free less-sodium chicken broth (about 3½ cups)

2½ cups bite-size chunks rotisserie chicken

1 medium tart apple, unpeeled and chopped

½ cup raisins

½ teaspoon salt

Hot rice

1. Lightly coat a Dutch oven with nonstick cooking spray. Heat the oil in the pan over medium heat. Add the onion and carrots, and stir to coat with the oil. Cook, stirring frequently, until the onion is clear and the carrots are slightly tender, 6–8 minutes.

2. Add the curry powder and garlic, and cook for 2 minutes, stirring constantly to prevent burning. Sprinkle the flour over all and stir just until the flour blends in. The mixture will not be smooth. Slowly add the broth to the pan, stirring constantly. Raise the heat to medium-high and bring the mixture to a boil, stirring constantly. Lower the heat to medium and simmer until the sauce thickens slightly, 6–8 minutes, stirring frequently.

3. Stir in the chicken, apple, raisins, and salt. Cover the pan, turn the heat to low, and simmer, stirring frequently to prevent sticking, until the mixture is hot and bubbly and has thickened slightly, about 10 minutes. Serve over rice.

▶ Note

- Freeze any leftover curry with the rice for up to one month for a quick lunch or dinner.

Company's Coming: Since this is a good choice for entertaining, make extra batches a day ahead and refrigerate. Reheat in the microwave or on the stove top, adding a little broth if necessary.

NOT ORDINARY CHICKEN À LA KING

—Makes 4 servings—

This rotisserie chicken version of the popular sherry-laced dish bears no resemblance to cafeteria food of old. Ready-to-use cream soup makes short order of this soothing favorite by offering the convenience of a creamy sauce in a can. A must in everyone's repertoire, this is a great quick family meal that dresses up nicely for company.

SPICE BLEND

1 teaspoon dried thyme, crumbled between the fingers
¼ teaspoon pepper
Pinch of ground nutmeg

BASE

3 tablespoons butter
1 large green bell pepper, chopped (about 1 cup)
½ medium onion, finely chopped (about ½ cup)
1 (6-ounce) package already-sliced mushrooms (about 2 cups)
1 teaspoon jarred minced garlic
1 (10¾-ounce) can condensed cream of chicken soup, undiluted

¾ cup milk
¼ cup dry sherry
2 cups bite-size chunks rotisserie chicken
1 (4-ounce) jar diced pimientos, drained (about ½ cup)
1 tablespoon finely chopped flat-leaf (Italian) parsley
Toast points, biscuits, or baked frozen puff pastry shells

1. **MAKE THE SPICE BLEND:** Stir the ingredients together in a small bowl and set aside.

2. **MAKE THE BASE:** Melt the butter in a 12-inch nonstick skillet over medium heat. Add the bell pepper and onion, and cook, stirring frequently, until the pepper begins to soften, about 5 minutes. Add the mushrooms and garlic, sprinkle with the spice blend, and cook, stirring constantly, until the mushrooms begin to lose their juices, about 3 minutes. Stir in the soup, milk, and sherry. When the soup melts, stir in the chicken and pimientos, and bring to a simmer, stirring frequently. Turn the heat to low and simmer for 10 minutes, stirring frequently. Remove from the heat, stir in the parsley, and spoon over toast, biscuits, or puff pastry shells.

▶ Note

- White toast cut on the diagonal or biscuits are perfect for family. Buttery puff pastry shells make an elegant presentation for a dinner party.

Food Fact

- Theories abound on the origins of this American mainstay, with credit ranging from a hotel in London in the late 1800s to its first appearance being in Long Island, New York, in the 1920s. There seems to be agreement on what matters: that chicken à la king is a delicious blend of chopped chicken and vegetables in a cream sauce, finished off with a splash of sherry.

Feeling Flush: Use 2 cups of sliced wild mushrooms for a luxurious touch.

Lighter Touch: Use the reduced fat, less-sodium variety of soup and 2% milk.

Company's Coming: This makes great "help yourself" buffet fare. Make several batches and spoon into a slow cooker or chafing dish. Offer several bread choices on a platter and let guests help themselves.

STIR-FRY CHICKEN

—Makes 4 servings—

The veggies are on the table in no time flat with the convenience of a rotisserie chicken and frozen stir-fry vegetables. I like the crispness that comes with a few quick chops of fresh vegetables, so I add them to the already frozen mix. Start the rice as soon as you walk into the kitchen so it will be ready at the same time as your delicious Chinese-style stir-fry.

3 tablespoons oil

1 large rib celery, sliced on the diagonal into ½-inch slices

½ *each* red bell pepper and green bell pepper, cut into ¼-inch-wide strips

2 teaspoons *each* jarred minced garlic and jarred chopped ginger

1 (16-ounce) package frozen stir-fry vegetables

1 (15-ounce) can baby sweet corn, *not pickled,* drained

2 tablespoons water

½ cup bean sprouts

1 tablespoon dark sesame oil

2½ cups large shreds rotisserie chicken, pulled apart by hand

½ cup bottled stir-fry sauce

Hot rice or ramen noodles prepared without flavor packets

1. Heat the oil in a 12-inch nonstick skillet over medium-high heat. Add the celery and cook for 2 minutes, stirring frequently. Add the bell peppers, garlic, and ginger, and cook 2 more minutes, stirring frequently. The peppers will be crisp.

2. Add the frozen stir-fry mix, corn, and water. Cook, stirring frequently, until the stir-fry mix begins to soften and the mixture is hot, about 5 minutes. Add the bean sprouts and sesame oil, stir well, and cook for 1 minute. Add the chicken and the sauce, and cook, stirring frequently, just long enough to heat through, about 2 minutes. Serve immediately over hot rice or cooked and drained ramen noodles.

Produce Pick: Look for bean sprouts that are crisp when you snap them and have no dark ends.

Lighter Touch: If you go easy on the rice, this is a nice light meal.

Just You or Two: Cut the recipe in half.

Serve It Up: Make it a Chinese restaurant night. Put out chopsticks and store-bought fortune cookies and have fun.

CHICKEN CROQUETTES

—Makes 4 servings—

This is my rotisserie chicken version of one of my favorite pantry meals growing up, Salmon Croquettes. The soda crackers work with the Old Bay seasoning, and Worcestershire sauce brings a southern touch. The sauce is in the style of the classic French rémoulade. It adds a nice finish and a bit of spice.

SAUCE

½ cup mayonnaise
¼ cup chopped roasted red pepper
1 tablespoon sweet pickle relish, drained

2 teaspoons sweet paprika
Squirt of freshly-squeezed lemon juice
Pinch of cayenne (optional)

CROQUETTES

2½ cups small shreds rotisserie chicken, skin removed (some dark meat preferred)
½ bunch green onions, sliced (about ½ cup)
½ red bell pepper, finely chopped (about ½ cup)
3 tablespoons mayonnaise
2 tablespoons finely chopped flat-leaf (Italian) parsley

1 tablespoon Old Bay seasoning
2 teaspoons freshly-squeezed lemon juice
2 teaspoons Worcestershire sauce
1 teaspoon jarred minced garlic
20 individual soda crackers with unsalted tops (about 1¾ × 1¾ inches each)
1 egg, beaten with a pinch of salt

2 tablespoons vegetable oil, divided

1. **MAKE THE SAUCE:** Stir the ingredients together in a small bowl and set aside.

2. **MAKE THE CROQUETTES:** Toss together the chicken, onion, bell pepper, mayonnaise, parsley, Old Bay seasoning, lemon juice, Worcestershire sauce, and garlic in a medium bowl. Crumble the crackers over the mixture, making fine crumbs. Pour the egg over all and toss well to combine. Use a ⅓ cup measure to scoop up the mixture. Form oval croquettes about 3 inches long by ¾-inch high by putting the mixture between the palms of your hands and pressing down firmly but gently.

3. Heat 1 tablespoon oil in a 12-inch nonstick skillet over medium heat. Add the croquettes and cook until golden brown on one side, about 4 minutes. Turn and cook until the other side turns a light brown and the tops of the croquettes are firm to the touch, about 2 minutes. Press down gently with the spatula and add more oil as needed. Serve immediately with a dollop of sauce.

▶ Notes

- Old Bay seasoning is a wonderfully complex blend of spices and seasonings ranging from celery seed to mace. Look for it in yellow cans.
- I have one less bowl to wash because I mix these in the dome of the chicken container. Then I toss the container.

Do-Ahead Tip: Mix everything together ahead of time except the egg and cracker crumbs. Pop the mixture in the fridge and stir in the crackers and eggs at cooking time.

Company's Coming: Make bite-size "chicken cakes" by scooping out about 2 tablespoons of mixture and cooking until golden on each side. Arrange on a serving platter and top each with a small dollop of sauce for a terrific appetizer.

QUICK COQ AU VIN

—Makes 4 servings—

What an indulgence! You can serve coq au vin anytime you are in the mood when you start with a rotisserie chicken. I get this to the table even faster by simmering the wine while the vegetables are cooking. There is no need to buy expensive wine; I use a modestly priced merlot. Do choose a bottle that you would be happy to drink since the flavor is key to this dish.

WINE MIXTURE

2½ cups dry red wine, such as merlot
1 large shallot, peeled and smashed
4 sprigs flat-leaf (Italian) parsley
2 bay leaves

SPICE BLEND

1½ teaspoons dried thyme, crumbled between the fingers
1 teaspoon salt
½ teaspoon pepper

BASE

4 slices bacon
2 tablespoons butter
1 cup frozen pearl onions (about half of a 5-ounce bag)
10 baby carrots, cut lengthwise into quarters
8 medium-size button mushrooms, cut into quarters
2 teaspoons jarred minced garlic

1 rotisserie chicken, cut into serving pieces
½ cup fat-free less-sodium chicken broth
3 tablespoons finely chopped flat-leaf (Italian) parsley

Lightly buttered noodles or boiled red potatoes

1. **MAKE THE WINE MIXTURE:** Combine the ingredients in a small saucepan and bring to a boil over medium heat. Turn the heat to low and simmer, uncovered, for 15 minutes while you prepare the rest of the dish.

2. **MAKE THE SPICE BLEND:** Stir the ingredients together in a small bowl and set aside.

3. **MAKE THE BASE:** Cook the bacon until crisp in a nonaluminum Dutch oven over medium heat. Drain on a paper towel and remove all but 2 tablespoons of the drippings from the pan. Return the pan to the stove over medium heat. Add the butter, onions, and carrots, and cook, stirring frequently, until the onions begin to soften, about 5 minutes. Add the mushrooms and garlic, and cook, stirring frequently, until the mushrooms lose their juice and the onions turn golden brown, about 5 minutes. Sprinkle the spice blend over all and cook for 1 minute, stirring constantly.

4. Place the chicken on top of the vegetables. Pour in the broth, and the hot wine mixture, leaving the bay leaves in the pot. Simmer, uncovered, for 10 minutes, stirring occasionally. Crumble the bacon into the Dutch oven, stir well, and simmer 5 more minutes. Remove the shallot and parsley sprigs and discard. Place the chicken in a serving bowl, stir the chopped parsley into the juices, and spoon over the chicken. Serve over noodles or potatoes.

▶ Note
- Coq au vin has a purplish hue from the red wine, so do not be alarmed.

Company's Coming: You can make this a day ahead and reheat it at serving time. Stir in the bacon and parsley when reheating.

CHICKEN MOLE

—Makes 4 servings—

A skillet and creative blending of everyday ingredients transform an everyday rotisserie chicken into a sumptuous, richly flavored meal from the heart of Mexico. Round out the meal with baby carrots and a romaine salad.

SPICE BLEND

2 tablespoons *unsweetened* baking cocoa powder

4 teaspoons mild chili powder

1 teaspoon ground cinnamon

½ teaspoon dried oregano, crumbled between the fingers

½ teaspoon salt

¼ teaspoon cayenne

Pinch of nutmeg

SAUCE

2 tablespoons vegetable oil

1 large onion, thinly sliced (about 1 cup)

1 (4-ounce) can diced mild chiles

1 tablespoon jarred minced garlic

1 (14½-ounce) can fat-free less-sodium chicken broth (about 1¾ cups)

1 tablespoon cornstarch mixed with ¼ cup cold water

2 tablespoons creamy peanut butter

1 rotisserie chicken, cut into serving pieces

3 tablespoons finely chopped cilantro

Hot steamed rice and warm corn tortillas

1. **MAKE THE SPICE BLEND:** Stir the ingredients together in a small bowl and set aside.

2. **MAKE THE SAUCE:** Heat the oil in a 12-inch nonstick skillet over medium heat. Add the onion and cook, stirring frequently, until the slices turn gold, 8–10 minutes. Add the chiles, garlic, and spice blend, and cook for 2 minutes, stirring constantly. Stir in the broth. Stir the cornstarch mixture, then add it to the skillet along with the peanut butter, and bring to a boil, stirring frequently. Turn the heat to low, add the chicken, and spoon the sauce over the chicken. Simmer, uncovered, for 15 minutes, stirring frequently. Stir in the cilantro. Serve over hot rice with tortillas.

▶ Note

- There are as many versions of mole as there are cooks. A weekend spent assisting the renowned chef of Mexican cuisine Diana Kennedy taught me firsthand that moles have a wonderful range of flavors, from the chile and chocolate-based mole poblano—from which this recipe hails—to lettuce and nut-based moles.

In a Pinch: Pour 2 cups canned ready-to-use mole sauce over the cooked onions and stir in the chicken.

Play It Again: Shred the leftover chicken and stir together with the sauce. Fill warmed corn tortillas and top with chopped tomatoes for mole tacos or spoon into a burrito-size flour tortilla along with rice and beans for a quick burrito.

Company's Coming: You can make this a day ahead and reheat it at serving time.

RUB-YOUR-TUMMY POTATOES O'BRIEN

—Makes 4 servings—

One of the most popular breakfast restaurants in our area serves skillet after skillet of their version of this pleasing dish. I jump-start my recipe with convenient frozen potatoes O'Brien and liven them up with a quick chop of green onions. The name comes from our older son's reaction the first time he tasted these. Your reaction will probably be very close.

SPICE BLEND

2 teaspoons paprika
1 teaspoon salt
¾ teaspoon pepper

POTATOES

¼ cup vegetable oil
1 (28-ounce) package frozen potatoes O'Brien (about 6¾ cups)
2 cups bite-size chunks rotisserie chicken
1 cup bite-size chunks deli ham
1 small bunch green onions, thinly sliced (about ¾ cup)

⅓ cup fat-free less-sodium chicken broth or water
1 tablespoon jarred minced garlic
⅔ cup already-shredded mild Cheddar cheese
Tomato slices

1. **MAKE THE SPICE BLEND:** Stir the ingredients together in a small bowl and set aside.

2. **MAKE THE POTATOES:** Heat the oil in a 12-inch nonstick skillet over medium-high heat. Add the potatoes and cook for 5 minutes, stirring frequently and turning the potatoes over. Add the spice blend and cook until the potatoes just begin to soften, about 4 minutes more. Add the

chicken, ham, onions, broth, and garlic, and stir well. Cook until the potatoes are soft, the moisture has evaporated, and the mixture is heated through, about 3 minutes. Remove from the heat and stir in the cheese. Serve immediately with tomato slices.

▶ Note

- If you are so inclined, top these with a fried or scrambled egg, as the restaurant does. I like them as is.

CHICKEN CREOLE

—Makes 4 servings—

One of my favorite dishes as a child was my mother's special-occasion Friday-night Shrimp Creole. I have re-created the rich tomato flavors laced with onion, green bell pepper, and spices that I so loved, but this time with an at-the-ready rotisserie chicken. My version is less expensive but no less delicious. Start the rice first so it will be ready when the Chicken Creole is.

2 tablespoons butter
2 tablespoons olive oil
1 large onion, chopped (about 1 cup)
1 large green bell pepper, chopped (about 1 cup)
2 ribs celery, sliced in half lengthwise and then cut crosswise into thin slices
1 tablespoon jarred minced garlic
2 tablespoons salt-free creole seasoning, plus more to taste

2½–3 cups bite-size chunks rotisserie chicken
1 (28-ounce) can crushed tomatoes in purée
½ cup water
2 tablespoons Worcestershire sauce
2 bay leaves
¾ teaspoon salt

Hot rice
½ bunch green onions, thinly sliced (about ½ cup)

1. Heat the butter and oil in a Dutch oven or soup pot over medium-high heat. When the butter melts, add the onion, bell pepper, and celery, and cook, stirring frequently, until the vegetables just begin to soften, about 6 minutes. Add the garlic and cook 2 more minutes, stirring constantly. Add the 2 tablespoons creole seasoning and cook for 1 minute, stirring constantly. Add the chicken, tomatoes, water, Worcestershire sauce, bay leaves, and salt. Stir well and bring to a boil, stirring frequently. Turn the heat to low and simmer, covered, for 15 minutes to heat through and blend the flavors, stirring frequently. Add more creole seasoning if desired.

2. Remove the bay leaves. Spoon the chicken creole over the hot rice and sprinkle with the onions.

- Onion, green bell pepper, and celery are the foundation of many a Creole dish.
- I like to use salt-free creole seasoning so that I can choose how much salt to add. Omit the salt in the recipe if you use a seasoning that already has salt in it. Creole seasonings also vary in spiciness, so add more if you like it spicier.

Do-Ahead Tip: This reheats quite well, so you can easily make it the day before.

Company's Coming: My mother served her Shrimp Creole in little casserole dishes nestled in rattan, a nice upscale touch. Consider individual serving dishes for a wonderful company dinner that you can make a day ahead.

INDIAN CHICKEN IN TOMATO CREAM SAUCE

—Makes 4 servings—

———— ⸙ ————

A rotisserie chicken stands in quite well for the original tandoori chicken in this version of the simple north Indian dish known as Butter Chicken. In just a few simple steps with a handful of spices, an ordinary chicken becomes an exotic, family-pleasing meal with a richly spiced sauce that melds right into the chicken. The dish is done when the meat is—as Indian cookbook author Julie Sahni describes it—"meltingly tender." Serve spinach, quickly cooked in oil and garlic to complete the meal.

SPICE BLEND

1 tablespoon garam masala seasoning (see Note)

1½ teaspoons ground ginger

½ teaspoon ground cinnamon

¼ teaspoon cayenne

SAUCE

3 tablespoons butter

1 large onion, chopped (about 1 cup)

2 teaspoons jarred minced garlic

1 tablespoon tomato paste

1 (15-ounce) can tomato sauce

1 (14½-ounce) can diced tomatoes in juice

1 rotisserie chicken, cut into serving pieces and skin removed

1 (10-ounce) box frozen peas, placed in a colander and run under hot water to thaw

⅓ cup heavy (whipping) cream

Hot basmati rice

Pita bread, warmed according to package directions

1. **MAKE THE SPICE BLEND:** Stir the ingredients together in a small bowl and set aside.

2. **MAKE THE SAUCE:** Melt the butter in a 12-inch nonstick skillet over medium heat. Add the onion and cook, stirring frequently, until the pieces just begin to turn gold, about 5 minutes. Add the garlic, tomato paste, and spice blend, and cook for 1 minute, stirring constantly to prevent burning. The spices will be fragrant. Add the tomato sauce and diced tomatoes, and stir well. Add the chicken pieces, spoon the sauce over the top, and bring to a simmer. Turn the heat to low and cook, uncovered, until the chicken is warmed through and the sauce is flavorful, about 10 minutes. Stir frequently. Remove the chicken to a serving dish and cover to keep warm.

3. Shake any excess water from the peas. Add the peas and cream to the sauce in the pan, stir well, and heat through. Do not boil. Spoon the sauce over the chicken. Serve with rice and warmed pita bread.

VARIATION

If you prefer shreds of chicken to whole pieces, remove the skin from the chicken and pull the meat into large chunks by hand. Add to the pan along with the garlic, tomato paste, and spice blend. Cook for 3 minutes and then add the tomato sauce and continue with the recipe. Serve over basmati rice.

▶ Note

- Garam masala, a blend of fragrant spices, is a mainstay in Indian cuisine. Indian cooks often mix their own custom blends. Good, bottled all-purpose versions are available in the supermarket. If you have a choice, select a variety that does not have salt as the top ingredient.

Lighter Touch: Stir in plain yogurt instead of the heavy cream. The sauce will be tangier and less rich, but it will still be delicious.

Company's Coming: This great company dish says you labored away when you really did not have to.

SLOW-COOKER SMOTHERED CHICKEN

—Makes 4 servings—

Chicken smothered in cream of mushroom soup is always welcome at my table. With my slow cooker and a rotisserie chicken ready, I can quickly layer the ingredients and come back a few hours later to an enticing smell and a delicious creamy meal. I used an oval pot for this dish.

SAUCE

1 (10¾-ounce) can condensed cream of
   mushroom soup, undiluted
½ soup can of milk
2 teaspoons jarred minced garlic
1 teaspoon dried thyme, crumbled between
   the fingers

1 teaspoon paprika
¼ teaspoon pepper
1 bay leaf

BASE

1 large onion, sliced crosswise into ¼-inch slices
1 rotisserie chicken, cut into serving pieces
1 (6-ounce) package sliced mushrooms (about 2 cups)

Hot rice

1. **MAKE THE SAUCE:** Stir the ingredients together in a one-quart measuring cup, being careful not to break up the bay leaf.

2. **MAKE THE BASE:** Place the onion in the slow cooker, followed by the chicken and then the mushrooms. Pour the sauce over the chicken and cook on low for 4–5 hours, until the flavors have blended and the sauce is thick and bubbly. Remove the bay leaf and discard. Serve over hot rice.

Feeling Flush: Use your favorite blend of wild mushrooms.

Lighter Touch: Use the reduced-fat less-sodium variety of soup.

SNAPPY SMOTHERED CHICKEN

—Makes 4 servings—

A rotisserie chicken lets me serve an American favorite, soup-smothered chicken, in no time flat. The mushrooms simmer long enough to meld right into the creamy sauce. I love this over hot rice, but noodles are also good. Serve green beans and cherry tomatoes alongside.

SPICE BLEND

1 teaspoon paprika
1 teaspoon dried thyme, crumbled between the fingers
¼ teaspoon pepper

CHICKEN

3 tablespoons butter
1 large onion, chopped (about 1 cup)
1 (6-ounce) package sliced mushrooms (about 2 cups)
2 teaspoons jarred minced garlic
1 (10¾-ounce) can condensed cream of mushroom soup, undiluted

1 soup can of milk
1 rotisserie chicken, cut into serving pieces

Hot rice or cooked wide egg noodles

1. **MAKE THE SPICE BLEND:** Stir the ingredients together in a small bowl and set aside.

2. **MAKE THE CHICKEN:** Melt the butter in a 12-inch nonstick skillet over medium-high heat. Add the onion and mushrooms, and cook, stirring frequently, until the onion starts to

soften and the mushrooms start to lose their juice, about 4 minutes. Add the garlic and sprinkle the spice blend over all. Cook for 2 minutes, stirring constantly. Stir in the soup and milk, and bring to a boil, stirring frequently. Add the chicken and spoon the sauce over the top. Turn the heat to low and simmer, covered, until the chicken is heated through, and the sauce flavors have come together, 10–15 minutes, stirring frequently. Serve over rice or noodles.

Lighter Touch: Try reduced-fat less-sodium variety of soup and 1% milk.

CHICKEN CACCIATORE

—Makes 4–6 servings—

This is high on my list of satisfying, feel-good meals that take very little effort. I serve this when everyone has had a long day and we want a bit of cozy comfort on our plates. Round out the meal with a green salad, warm crusty bread, and your favorite wine or sparkling beverage.

SPICE BLEND

2 tablespoons dried Italian herb seasoning, crumbled between the fingers
1 teaspoon salt
¼ teaspoon pepper

SAUCE

3 tablespoons olive oil
1 large onion, thinly sliced (about 1 cup)
1 large green bell pepper, chopped (about 1 cup)
1 (8-ounce) package sliced mushrooms (about 2½ cups)
1 tablespoon jarred minced garlic
1 (28-ounce) can crushed tomatoes in purée

½ cup fat-free less-sodium chicken broth
½ cup dry white wine
2 bay leaves
1 rotisserie chicken, cut into serving pieces

12 ounces spaghetti, cooked according to package directions and kept warm

1. **MAKE THE SPICE BLEND:** Stir the ingredients together in a small bowl and set aside.

2. **MAKE THE SAUCE:** Lightly coat a Dutch oven with nonstick cooking spray. Add the oil and warm over medium-high heat. Add the onion, bell pepper, and mushrooms. Cook, stirring

frequently, until the onion is clear and the pepper is soft, about 4 minutes. Add the garlic and spice blend, and cook for 2 minutes, stirring constantly.

3.   Add the tomatoes, broth, wine, and bay leaves. Stir well and bring to a simmer, stirring frequently. Add the chicken, turn the heat to medium-low, and simmer, covered, until the mixture thickens and is heated through, about 15 minutes. Stir occasionally. Remove the bay leaves. Spoon the sauce over the spaghetti, place the chicken pieces on top, and serve immediately.

VARIATION

Chicken Cacciatore Spaghetti:

Remove and discard the chicken skin, pull the meat into large chunks, and stir it into the sauce. Spoon over the spaghetti. Sprinkle with already-shredded Parmesan cheese.

In a Pinch: Substitute 1 cup of fat-free less-sodium chicken broth for the broth and wine.

ROASTED CHICKEN MOZZARELLA FINGERS

—Makes 2–3 servings—

A rotisserie chicken gets this kids' favorite, Chicken Parmesan, on the table in a hurry without the hassle of handling raw chicken. Serve with green beans or lightly sautéed zucchini rounds and garlic toast for a meal you will get requests for again and again.

½ cup dry Italian-seasoned bread crumbs

2 large rotisserie chicken breast halves (about ½ pound), skin removed

1 large egg, beaten with 1 tablespoon water

1 (14-ounce) jar pasta sauce (about 1½ cups)

Already-shredded mozzarella cheese, to taste

Cooked spaghetti

1. Preheat the oven to 400° F. Lightly coat an 11 × 7-inch pan with nonstick cooking spray.

2. Place the bread crumbs on a plate. Slice the chicken into ¼-inch diagonal slices, cutting with the grain to keep the pieces together. Pour the egg and water mixture into a medium bowl. Dip the chicken into the egg mixture, one half at a time, letting any excess egg drip back into the bowl. Place the chicken in the bread crumbs and sprinkle the bread crumbs over the top and sides of the chicken, pressing down gently to make the crumbs stick. Place in a single layer in the prepared pan. Bake until the bread crumbs are lightly toasted and the chicken is firm to the touch, about 10 minutes.

3. Remove the pan from the oven. Pour the pasta sauce over the chicken and sprinkle with cheese, as desired. Return to the oven and bake until the cheese melts and the sauce is bubbly, about 7 minutes. Serve over cooked spaghetti.

Double Duty: This recipe doubles well. Bake the strips in a 9 × 13-inch pan and keep the drumsticks for a special lunch box treat. Or use the rest of the meat for a stew or salad.

Serve It Up: Serve on toasted French rolls with salad alongside for a good lunch.

SALSA-STUFFED BELL PEPPERS
WITH CHIPOTLE SAUCE

—Makes 4–6 servings—

These peppers are a busy cook's dream: quick, tasty, and colorful. Red bell peppers add a sweetness that appeals to diners who might find green peppers a little harsh. This recipe is a perfect use for leftover brown rice, but you can also quickly cook instant brown rice if you don't have any cooked rice on hand.

3 large red bell peppers, cut in half lengthwise and seeds removed

SPICE BLEND

½ teaspoon ground cumin
½ teaspoon garlic powder

½ teaspoon salt
¼ teaspoon pepper

FILLING

2½ cups cooked brown rice (scant 1 cup uncooked rice)
1 cup bite-size chunks rotisserie chicken
¾ cup salsa
½ cup rinsed and drained canned black beans

½ cup frozen or canned corn kernels
½ cup already-shredded Monterey Jack cheese
½ bunch green onions, thinly sliced (about ½ cup)

SAUCE

¾ cup light sour cream
1 to 2 tablespoons finely chopped chipotle pepper in adobo sauce
¼ teaspoon salt

1. Preheat the oven to 350° F. Lightly coat a 13 × 9-inch pan with nonstick cooking spray. Set aside. Place the bell peppers in a small microwaveable dish, cut side up. Add about ¼-inch of water to the pan, cover, and microwave on high just until the peppers begin to soften, about 3 minutes. Do not overcook. Remove from the pan, turn the peppers upside down, and shake out any water. Place the peppers, cut side up, in the prepared pan.

2. **MAKE THE SPICE BLEND:** Stir the ingredients together in a medium bowl.

3. **MAKE THE FILLING:** Stir the filling ingredients and the spice blend together in a medium bowl. Mound the filling in the peppers, pressing down lightly and rounding the top. Bake, uncovered, until the filling is hot and the peppers are tender, about 30 minutes.

4. **MAKE THE SAUCE:** Meanwhile, stir the sauce ingredients together. Drizzle over the hot peppers.

▶ Note

- Leftover chipotle peppers will keep for one month in a covered glass container in the refrigerator. Freeze for longer storage.

Company's Coming: These are pretty enough for company and are great for showers or buffets.

CHICKEN À LA PAPRIKASH

—Makes 4 servings—

—— 🥄🍴 ——

Paprika is the essence of this Hungarian-style dish, so make sure your paprika is fresh. I store mine in the refrigerator. Although not traditional, the squeeze of ketchup adds another touch of sweetness and a subtle hint of tomato.

SPICE BLEND

2 tablespoons paprika
½ teaspoon salt

¼ teaspoon ground ginger
¼ teaspoon ground nutmeg

CHICKEN

2 tablespoons vegetable oil
2 large onions, cut in half and thinly sliced (about 2 cups)
2 teaspoons jarred minced garlic
2 tablespoons all-purpose flour
1¼ cups fat-free less-sodium chicken broth

¼ cup light sour cream, at room temperature
1 tablespoon ketchup
1 rotisserie chicken, cut into serving pieces, skin removed
Hot buttered wide egg noodles, cooked according to package directions and kept warm

1. **MAKE THE SPICE BLEND:** Stir the ingredients together in a small bowl and set aside.

2. **MAKE THE CHICKEN:** Heat the oil in a 12-inch nonstick skillet over medium heat. Add the onions and cook, stirring frequently, until they begin to turn golden brown, about 10 minutes. Add the garlic and sprinkle the spice blend over all. Stir well and cook for 2 minutes, stirring constantly. Stir the flour into the broth. Add to the skillet, stir well, and bring to a boil. Turn the heat to low and simmer, covered, until the mixture thickens slightly, about 4 minutes, stirring occasionally. Stir in the sour cream and ketchup. Add the chicken, spoon the sauce over the top, and simmer, covered, for 10 minutes, stirring frequently. Do not boil. Serve over the buttered egg noodles.

SLOW-COOKING MEXICAN RAGÙ

—Makes 4–6 servings—

What a treat awaits you with this simple dish that cooks as you go about your day. The slow cooking transforms basic ingredients into a sumptuous and versatile ragù. I enjoy the richly flavored juices so much that I serve this on crumbled corn muffins to soak up every last drop.

SPICE BLEND

1½ teaspoons chili powder
½ teaspoon ground cumin
½ teaspoon salt

RAGÙ

3½–4 cups large chunks rotisserie chicken, pulled apart by hand
1 (16-ounce) jar chipotle salsa (about 2 cups)
1 (14½-ounce) can cream-style corn
1 (10¾-ounce) can condensed Cheddar cheese soup, undiluted

1 large onion, chopped (about 1 cup)
1 cup already-shredded Mexican blend cheese (4 ounces)
1 cup fat-free less-sodium chicken broth
1 (2¼-ounce) can sliced ripe black olives, drained (about ½ cup)

ACCOMPANIMENTS

Store-bought corn muffins or polenta log
Light sour cream, to taste
Chopped cilantro, to taste

1. **MAKE THE SPICE BLEND:** Mix the ingredients together in a small bowl and set aside.

2. **MAKE THE RAGÙ:** Combine the ingredients in a slow cooker. Add the spice blend and stir well. Cover and cook on low or medium-low heat for 5 hours. The mixture will be quite hot and the flavors will be blended.

3. To serve, break a corn muffin into each bowl, and spoon the ragù on top. Or pan-cook polenta slices according to package directions and top with the ragù. Garnish as desired.

▶ Note

- If your slow cooker has a medium-low setting, use it. Otherwise, set the pot on low. I use a 4-quart round pot for this. Remember not to take the lid off while the dish is cooking, or you will let precious heat escape and your cooking time will be longer.

Company's Coming: Great for potlucks. Pack it up right in the pot, and it will still be hot when you get there. This also makes a really good dip when served with sturdy tortilla chips.

Shopping Tip: Some stores stock polenta in the refrigerator case in the deli, and others keep it on the shelf near the pasta. Ask the manager if you don't spot it.

Play It Again: If you have about 3 cups of ragù left over and a 24-ounce tube of polenta, you have a great Mexican lasagna in the making. Preheat the oven to 350° F. and lightly coat an 8 × 8-inch glass pan with nonstick cooking spray. Line the bottom with ½-inch slices of ready-to-heat polenta and then spread on the leftover ragù. Top with more slices of polenta, sprinkle with 1 cup already-shredded Mexican blend cheese, and bake in a 350° F oven until the cheese melts and the filling is bubbly, about 30 minutes.

KNOCKOUT NOODLES AND GLORIOUS GRAINS

Nothing is more natural than pairing pleasing pastas and good-for-you grains with a rotisserie chicken. With so many sauces, rices, grains, and pasta shapes to choose from you can keep your family's taste buds jumping. Some of the recipes in this chapter are good everyday American fare, such as the Chicken and Rice Divan. Others are newer to our tables like the Pineapple Fried Rice, made with fragrant jasmine rice, that I first tasted in a Thai restaurant. These meals are family pleasers when you want the starch and the rest of the dish all in one.

Go beyond the recipes in this chapter for pastas, and don't be afraid to pick the pasta of your choice. You can add some quick-chopped chicken and a ready-to-use fresh or frozen vegetable. Add bottled or refrigerated sauce, and your pasta dinner is served. With a rotisserie chicken, you can even serve a great yaki soba, the classic Japanese noodle dish. Just pick up a package of yaki soba noodles in the refrigerator case and cook according to package directions, adding slivers of rotisserie chicken and fresh or frozen stir-fry vegetables. Being creative with the ingredients you choose will give you great meals in no time—and a lot less expensively than eating out or buying prepared meals.

Rice bowls are convenient. The freezer cases in my local grocery stores sport new flavors almost every time I peek. You can easily make your own bowls and get just what you want at a fraction of the cost. Start with a rice that you like and the flavor you are looking for: jasmine, white, or brown. If you are short on time, use an instant rice. By all means don't forget the flavored rice mixes, such as Spanish rice or even the flavored instant grain couscous. Mound the rice in the bowl and top with chunks of chicken and the vegetables, beans, cheese, or sauces of your choice. In no time you have a rice bowl. If the ingredients need to be warmed, just use a microwaveable bowl and pop it in. Rice bowls reheat well, making them great lunch box meals.

You cannot lose when you use these versatile chickens to start a pasta or grain meal. So put the pot on to boil and get ready for a great meal!

CHICKEN TETRAZZINI

—Makes 4 generous servings—

——— 🥄🍴 ———

Turkey tetrazzini is typically post-Thanksgiving fare, but tetrazzini is far too good to have just once a year. Traditionally baked for a few minutes, this version is great right from the stovetop.

8 ounces uncooked spaghetti

SPICE BLEND

¼ teaspoon ground nutmeg
¼ teaspoon white pepper
½ teaspoon salt

SAUCE

3 tablespoons butter
1 (6-ounce) carton sliced mushrooms (about 2 cups)
3 large green onions, thinly sliced (about ½ cup)
1 teaspoon jarred minced garlic
1 (10¾-ounce) can condensed cream of chicken soup, undiluted
1 (10¾-ounce) can condensed cream of mushroom soup, undiluted

1 cup milk
3 cups bite-size chunks rotisserie chicken, skin removed
1 (10-ounce) package frozen peas and carrots, thawed and drained (about 2¼ cups)
2 tablespoons dry sherry
¾ cup already-shredded Parmesan cheese, divided

1. **MAKE THE PASTA:** Break the spaghetti in half and cook in a large pot according to package directions until just tender to the bite. Drain and return to the pot.

2. **MAKE THE SPICE BLEND:** Meanwhile, stir the ingredients together in a small bowl and set aside.

3. **MAKE THE SAUCE:** Melt the butter in a 12-inch nonstick skillet over medium-high heat. Add the mushrooms and cook, stirring constantly, until they begin to soften, about 3 minutes. Add the onions and garlic, and cook, stirring constantly, until the onions are limp, about 1 minute. Sprinkle with the spice blend, stir well, and cook for 2 minutes, stirring constantly. The mixture should be fragrant.

4. Lower the heat to medium and add the soups and milk and stir well. Cook, stirring frequently, until the soups melt and the mixture comes to a simmer, about 5 minutes. Stir in the chicken, peas and carrots, sherry, and ½ cup cheese. Simmer, stirring constantly, until the chicken is hot and the cheese melts, about 4 minutes.

5. Spoon the hot chicken mixture over the pasta. Use tongs or two spoons to toss. Serve immediately, passing the additional ¼ cup cheese at the table.

▶ Food Fact
- As Italian as the name sounds, this all-American comfort food is truly all-American. Legend has it that Chicken Tetrazzini was created in San Francisco early in the 1900s in honor of the famous opera singer Luisa Tetrazzini. Campbell's Soup Company popularized tetrazzini with their version using Campbell's soup.

> **Feeling Flush:** You can jazz this up a bit by using 2 cups of your favorite wild mushrooms. They will cost you a little more, but the flavor will be more exotic.

Lighter Touch: Use the reduced-fat less-sodium varieties of the soups and 1% milk. The dish will be slightly less rich but every bit as good.

Just You or Two: This does not freeze well. However, you can create a different dish for day two. Simply put the leftovers in a buttered gratin dish, sprinkle with packaged dry bread crumbs mixed with a little grated Parmesan cheese, and bake in a 400° F oven until the sauce is bubbly and the cheese is brown.

CHICKEN AND RICE DIVAN

—Makes 4 generous servings—

This skillet version of Chicken Divan is creamy comfort at its best. The addition of rice to the classic dish makes it a quick meal-in-one that is easy to prepare and easy to serve. To save a little more time, buy bagged, ready-to-use broccoli florets or pick up florets at the salad bar. The broccoli, milk, and cheese make this a calcium-rich meal. Serve with tomato slices and a roll.

3 tablespoons butter
1 large onion, chopped (about 1 cup)
1 large red bell pepper, chopped (about 1 cup)
1 teaspoon jarred minced garlic
1 cup extra-long grain rice, not instant
1 teaspoon dried thyme, crumbled between the fingers
½ teaspoon salt
1 (14½-ounce) can fat-free less-sodium chicken broth (about 1¾ cups)

1 cup water
3 cups broccoli florets (about 10 ounces florets, or 1 pound broccoli with stems)
1 (10¾-ounce) can condensed cream of chicken soup, undiluted
1 soup can milk
2 cups bite-size chunks rotisserie chicken
1 cup already-shredded sharp Cheddar cheese

1. Melt the butter in a 12-inch nonstick skillet over medium heat. Add the onion, bell pepper, and garlic to the skillet. Cook until the bell pepper softens and the onions are clear, about 4 minutes, stirring frequently to prevent sticking.

2. Add the rice, thyme, and salt, stirring well to coat with the butter and to mix in the onion mixture. Cook for 3 minutes, stirring constantly. The rice should not brown. Add the broth and water. Stir well, bring to a boil, and turn the heat to low. Cover and cook until the rice begins to

soften, about 10 minutes, stirring occasionally. Add the broccoli florets, raise the heat to medium, and cook, uncovered, until the broccoli just begins to soften to the bite, about 5 minutes, stirring occasionally.

3. Stir in the soup and milk, and cook until the mixture is liquid, stirring frequently. Add the chicken, bring to a boil, and simmer, uncovered, until the mixture is heated through and the rice is tender, about 5 minutes, stirring occasionally. Remove from the heat and stir in the cheese.

▶ Food Fact

- Created in the 1930s in a now-defunct New York restaurant bearing the "Divan" name, Chicken Divan typically springs from the oven in a pan layered with broccoli spears, sliced poached chicken, and a sherry-spiked cheesy white sauce.

Lighter Touch: You can use a reduced-fat and less-sodium cream of chicken soup and 1% milk if you are watching your fat intake.

Company's Coming: Make this in batches for a great homey dinner or buffet table addition.

CHICKEN WITH RICE

(Arroz con Pollo)

—Makes 4–6 servings—

— 🥄🍴 —

One of my favorite versions of chicken and rice, this dish comes to mind whenever I think of easy everyday Mexican cooking. It is simple to prepare with ingredients you have on hand.

SPICE BLEND

1 teaspoon paprika
½ teaspoon dried oregano, crumbled between the fingers

½ teaspoon ground cumin
½ teaspoon dried parsley flakes
½ teaspoon salt

RICE

3 tablespoons olive oil
1 large onion, chopped (about 1 cup)
1 large green bell pepper, chopped (about 1 cup)
2 teaspoons jarred minced garlic
1 cup long-grain white rice
1 (16-ounce) jar chunky salsa
1 (14½-ounce) can fat-free less-sodium chicken broth (about 1¾ cups)

2 tablespoons tomato paste
2 bay leaves
½ cup frozen peas
1 rotisserie chicken, cut into serving pieces and skin removed
½ cup green olives with pimiento, coarsely chopped

1. **MAKE THE SPICE BLEND:** Stir the ingredients together in a small bowl and set aside.

2. Heat the oil in a 12-inch nonstick skillet over medium-high heat. Add the onion, bell pepper, and garlic, and cook, stirring frequently, until the onion and bell pepper are crisp-tender, about 4 minutes. Lower the heat to medium. Add the rice to the pan and stir well. Sprinkle the spice blend over all, stir well to combine, and cook for 2 minutes, stirring constantly. The spices should be fragrant.

3. Add the salsa, broth, and tomato paste to the pan. Stir well to combine. Add the bay leaves and bring the mixture to a boil. Turn the heat to low and cook, covered, for 10 minutes, stirring occasionally. Stir in the peas, and add the chicken pieces. Cook, uncovered, until almost all the moisture has been absorbed, about 8 minutes, stirring occasionally. Remove the bay leaves, stir in the olives, and serve.

GARLIC AND MUSHROOM SPAGHETTI

—Makes 4 servings—

This is one of my favorite dishes when I am in the mood for a simple dinner with quick and appetizingly clean flavors. Don't fret over the ¼ cup of olive oil; that is only one tablespoon a serving. Add toasted French bread and maybe a glass of your favorite white wine for a pleasurable meal that is great for the family or company.

8 ounces uncooked spaghetti, broken in half
½ cup of hot cooking water
¼ cup olive oil
3 tablespoons jarred minced garlic
1 (6-ounce) package sliced mushrooms (about 2 cups)
3 cups bite-size chunks rotisserie chicken
¼ cup capers, drained
¼ teaspoon salt, or to taste
½ teaspoon red pepper flakes (optional)
1 cup chopped Roma tomatoes (about 2 large tomatoes)
¾ cup already-shredded Parmesan cheese
2 tablespoons finely chopped flat-leaf (Italian) parsley

1. Cook the spaghetti according to package directions until firm to the bite. Use a ladle or glass measuring cup to carefully remove ½ cup of the hot water from the pot. Set aside. Drain the spaghetti and rinse in hot water, shaking off the excess. Set the spaghetti aside.

2. Combine the oil and garlic in a 12-inch nonstick skillet over medium heat. Cook, stirring frequently, until the garlic is fragrant, about 2 minutes. Add the mushrooms and cook, stirring frequently, until they begin to lose their juice and turn gold, about 4 minutes. Raise the heat to medium-high. Add the chicken, capers, salt, and red pepper flakes, if using. Stir well and cook for 2 minutes, stirring frequently. Add the reserved pasta liquid and then the spaghetti, and stir well to combine. Cook for 3 minutes to heat through, stirring frequently. Remove from the heat and stir in the tomatoes, cheese, and parsley. Serve immediately.

VARIATION

Garlic and Artichoke Spaghetti:

Drain the spaghetti without reserving any cooking liquid. Increase the capers to ⅓ cup. Add two 6-ounce jars of marinated artichoke hearts and their juices along with the chicken, capers, salt, and red pepper flakes. Continue as above, substituting ½ cup of dry vermouth for the hot cooking water.

Feeling Flush: Use a mix of your favorite wild mushrooms for a special treat.

TERIYAKI RICE BOWL

—Makes 4 servings—

The longest line in our local mall food court is always the Japanese restaurant that serves plate after plate of teriyaki chicken. My at-home rotisserie chicken version is far less expensive and just as good. And there is no need to stand in line. Start the rice as soon as you walk in the kitchen, and dinner is on the way. Serve a green salad alongside.

1 cup baby carrots, sliced crosswise into
   ¼-inch pieces
½ cup orange juice
1 (12-ounce) bottle teriyaki sauce (glaze, not
   marinade)
2½ cups bite-size chunks rotisserie chicken,
   skin removed

1 cup sliced mushrooms
1 large green onion, thinly sliced
4 cups hot rice

1. Put the carrots and the orange juice in a medium-size saucepan over medium heat. Bring to a simmer, and cook, covered, until the carrots are almost tender, about 5 minutes. Stir in the teriyaki sauce, chicken, and mushrooms. Bring to a boil and cook for 3 minutes, to soften the mushrooms, stirring frequently. Remove from the heat and stir in the onion.

2. Divide the rice among 4 bowls, forming a mound in the center. Ladle the chicken and teriyaki mixture over the rice and serve.

Lighter Touch: Cut back a little on the rice if you are watching calories.

ROASTED CHICKEN AND SAUSAGE JAMBALAYA

—Makes 4–6 servings—

Roasted chicken adds depth to the deliciously complex flavors while taking away preparation time in this delicious version of the Creole classic. Do not let the long list of ingredients deter you from adding this to your menu plans. Many of the ingredients are easy-to-measure spices or ready-to-use ingredients that add a lot of flavor but just a smidgen of preparation time. This reheats well, making it a great do-ahead company dish.

SPICE BLEND

2 teaspoons dried thyme, crumbled between the fingers

¼ teaspoon ground cumin

¼ teaspoon cayenne

¼ teaspoon salt, or to taste

RICE MIXTURE

2 tablespoons vegetable oil

1½ cups chopped onion (about 2 medium onions)

1 large green bell pepper, chopped (about 1 cup)

¾ cup finely chopped celery (about 2 small ribs)

1 cup long-grain white rice, not instant

2 teaspoons jarred minced garlic

2 (14½-ounce) cans fat-free less-sodium chicken broth (about 3½ cups)

1 (28-ounce) can diced tomatoes in juice

½ pound andouille or kielbasa sausage, cut into ½-inch chunks

3 tablespoons tomato paste

2 bay leaves

3 cups bite-size chunks rotisserie chicken

1. **MAKE THE SPICE BLEND:** Stir the ingredients together in a small bowl and set aside.

2. **MAKE THE RICE MIXTURE:** Lightly coat the bottom of a Dutch oven with nonstick cooking spray. Add the oil to the pan and heat for 1 minute. Add the onion, bell pepper, and celery, and cook, stirring frequently, until the onion is opaque and the vegetables are crisp-tender, 6–8 minutes. Add the rice, spice blend, and garlic, stirring to coat the rice with the spices. Cook for 1 minute, stirring constantly.

3. Stir in the broth, tomatoes, sausage, tomato paste, and bay leaves. Raise the heat to medium-high and bring the mixture to a boil, stirring frequently. Turn the heat to low and simmer, covered, until the rice is almost tender and the mixture has started to thicken, about 15 minutes. Stir frequently to prevent sticking.

4. Stir in the chicken. Continue cooking, covered, until the rice is tender and the mixture is creamy but not dry, 5–10 minutes, stirring occasionally. There should be a little liquid left. Remove the bay leaves and serve immediately.

▶ Notes

- Pass the cayenne at the table instead of adding it to the pot if you are serving tender tongues.
- Freeze any leftovers for up to one month.

Do-Ahead Tip: You can make this a day ahead, add a little chicken broth, and reheat it on the stove or in the microwave at serving time.

In a Pinch: Cook sausage along with onion, green pepper, and celery. Add to your favorite packaged jambalaya mix along with bite-size chunks of rotisserie chicken.

Company's Coming: Make two batches for a great buffet.

Serve It Up: For a meal that is hard to beat, serve with your favorite homemade or store-bought corn bread and a salad of hearts of romaine.

A LITTLE OF THIS, A LITTLE OF THAT CHICKEN FRIED RICE

—Makes 4 servings—

You can get this to the table faster than you can say, "Takeout, please." One of the beauties of this style of fried rice is that you can peek into the vegetable bin and pull out a little of this and a little of that to put it together. My vegetable selection is just a start. Experiment and do not hesitate to use the vegetables you have on hand. Just reach into the fridge and start cooking.

2 tablespoons vegetable oil
1 medium red bell pepper, chopped
1 cup sliced mushrooms
1 bunch green onions, thinly sliced
½ cup already-shredded carrots
1 tablespoon jarred minced garlic

2 teaspoons jarred chopped ginger
3–4 tablespoons light soy sauce
4 cups cooked rice, *not instant*, chilled
1½ cups large chunks rotisserie chicken, pulled apart by hand
1½ cups cooked small broccoli florets

1. Heat the oil in a 12-inch nonstick skillet over medium-high heat. Add the bell pepper and mushrooms, and cook, stirring frequently, until the bell pepper begins to soften and the mushrooms start to lose their juice, about 4 minutes. Add the onions, carrots, garlic, and ginger. Cook for 2 minutes, stirring constantly. The carrots will soften. Add the soy sauce, stir well, and then spoon in the rice. Stir well to combine. Add the chicken and broccoli, and cook for 3–4 minutes to heat through, stirring constantly. Serve immediately.

Quick Tip: Cook extra rice a day or two before, and you will be ready to put this together.

In a Pinch: Rice fries much better when it is chilled. If you do not have any leftover rice on hand and want this for dinner, you can quick-chill takeout rice. Lightly coat a baking sheet with nonstick cooking spray. Spread cool rice in the pan and pop it in the freezer while you pull everything else together.

TEX-MEX MAC AND CHEESE

—Makes 4 servings—

This macaroni cooks right in the skillet, and the flavors come together in a flash so that you can get this on the table in a hurry with just the skillet to wash. Serve sliced tomatoes and green beans or a salad alongside.

2 tablespoons butter
1⅓ cups small elbow macaroni
1¾ cups water
1 (12-ounce) can evaporated milk
1 teaspoon chili powder
1 teaspoon jarred minced garlic
½ teaspoon salt

1–2 cups already-shredded sharp Cheddar cheese
1½ cups bite-size chunks rotisserie chicken
1 (4-ounce) can mild diced green chiles, drained
3 large green onions, thinly sliced

1. Melt the butter in a 12-inch nonstick skillet over medium heat. Add the macaroni and cook for 2 minutes, stirring frequently. Add the water, evaporated milk, chili powder, garlic, and salt. Stir well. Bring to a boil and cook until the macaroni is tender, about 18 minutes. Stir frequently to prevent sticking and boil-overs, especially toward the end of the cooking time. There will be liquid remaining. Add cheese as desired stirring well to stop clumping, and then stir in the chicken, chiles, and onions. Cook for 1 minute to heat through. Serve immediately.

▶ Note
- You could stir in a little diced chipotle pepper and a touch of the adobo sauce instead of the chiles if you would like a hotter dish.

In a Pinch: Use 2 cups of large elbow macaroni if that is the size you have on hand; 1 cup of small macaroni weighs more than 1 cup of large macaroni.

Lighter Touch: Try reduced-fat cheese along with nonfat evaporated milk.

READY-in-MINUTES MACARONI and CHEESE

—Makes 4 servings—

If you are a fan of boxed mac and cheese, you will love this. A rotisserie chicken pairs with veggies to make that simple box a quick meal the kids will love. The shredded Cheddar cheese gives the dish a homemade touch. I serve a green salad and rolls alongside.

1 (7¼-ounce) box macaroni and cheese dinner
2 tablespoons butter
½ cup milk
1 cup frozen broccoli florets, thawed
1½ cups bite-size chunks rotisserie chicken

1 cup already-shredded Cheddar cheese
2 tablespoons diced pimientos, drained
½ teaspoon garlic powder
¼ teaspoon onion powder
Pepper, to taste

1. Prepare the macaroni and cheese according to package directions for the microwave, increasing the butter to 2 tablespoons and the milk to ½ cup. Stir them in at the end of the cooking time. Stir in the cheese sauce mix and broccoli. Add the chicken, cheese, pimientos, garlic powder, onion powder, and pepper, and stir well. Microwave, uncovered, on full power to heat through, about 2 minutes. Stir well and serve immediately.

CHOP SUEY AND RAMEN NOODLES

—Makes 4 servings—

The combination of ramen noodles, packaged chop suey mix, and a rotisserie chicken, of course, make this faster than takeout. Look for the chop suey mix, a combination of chopped Napa cabbage, bok choy, celery, and onions in the produce case with the bagged vegetables. I add carrots for a little color. This is great for a quick weeknight dinner or a lazy Saturday evening.

NOODLES

2 (14½-ounce) cans fat-free reduced-sodium chicken broth (about 3½ cups)
2 (3-ounce) packages ramen noodles, chicken flavor, 1 seasoning packet reserved for another use

CHOP SUEY

2 tablespoons vegetable oil
1 teaspoon jarred minced garlic
1 teaspoon jarred chopped ginger
1 (11 to 14-ounce) package fresh chop suey mix

½ cup already-shredded carrots
3 cups large chunks rotisserie chicken, pulled apart by hand
1 tablespoon water
1 tablespoon soy sauce, or to taste

1. **MAKE THE NOODLES:** Bring the broth to a boil in a medium saucepan over medium-high heat. Break the noodles in half, add to the boiling water, and stir. Cook just until tender, about 3 minutes, stirring occasionally. Drain immediately, rinse under hot water. Shake to remove excess water.

2. **MAKE THE CHOP SUEY:** Heat the vegetable oil in a 12-inch nonstick skillet over medium heat. Add the garlic, ginger, chop suey mix, and carrots. Stir well. Cook until the chop suey veg-

etables begin to soften, stirring frequently, about 3 minutes. Add the chicken, sprinkle the reserved seasoning packet and the water over all. Stir well and cook until heated through, 2–3 minutes, stirring frequently. Add the noodles to the skillet, stir and toss to combine with the vegetables, and heat just long enough to warm through, stirring frequently, about 2 minutes. Stir in the soy sauce and serve immediately.

▶ Note

- I use broth instead of water to cook the noodles for flavor without the salt of using both seasoning packets.

In a Pinch: Substitute a mixture of about 7 firmly-packed cups of chopped Napa cabbage, bok choy, onions, and celery for the chop suey mix. Or choose a stir fry mix with cabbage, onion, bok choy, and carrots.

ZUCCHINI AND TOMATO RISOTTO

—Makes 4–6 servings—

Risotto is one of my all-time favorite dishes. I used to labor over the stove, patiently adding the hot stock a little at a time to ensure the tender, creamy kernels of rice that mark a good risotto. Time is not on my side these days, but I still love risotto, so I start with a good packaged mix and quickly build a delicious main course that everyone loves. Serve with a green salad and crusty bread.

1 tablespoon olive oil

1 medium zucchini, trimmed and cut into ½-inch chunks

2 tablespoons butter

1 medium onion, chopped (about ¾ cup)

1 teaspoon jarred minced garlic

2 (5.2-ounce) boxes risotto Milanese-flavored rice mix

1 (14½-ounce) can fat-free less-sodium chicken broth (about 1¾ cups)

1¾ cups water

2 cups bite-size chunks rotisserie chicken

1 cup red grape tomatoes, cut in half

¾ cup already-shredded Parmesan cheese, plus more for serving, if desired

Salt, to taste

½ teaspoon white pepper

2 tablespoons finely chopped flat-leaf (Italian) parsley

1. Heat the oil in a 3-quart saucepan over medium heat. Add the zucchini and cook, stirring frequently, until it just begins to soften, about 3 minutes. Scoop into a bowl and set aside.

2. Return the pan to the stove over medium heat. Add the butter, onion, and garlic, and cook, stirring frequently, until the onion begins to soften, about 2 minutes. Add the rice mix, stir well to break up any clumps, and cook for 2 minutes, stirring constantly.

3. Raise the heat to medium-high, add the broth and water and bring to a boil, stirring occasionally. Turn the heat to low and simmer, partially covered, until the rice is almost tender and

most of the liquid is absorbed, about 15 minutes. Stir in the zucchini, chicken, tomatoes, cheese, salt, and pepper. Cover. Cook until heated through, about 3 more minutes, stirring frequently. Stir in the parsley. Serve, sprinkling with additional cheese if desired.

Play It Again: This reheats well.

Company's Coming: This makes a good, quick company meal when paired with a glass of wine.

SPEEDY SKILLET PAELLA

—Makes 4–6 servings—

———— 🥄🍴 ————

I have loved paella since I first tasted it, when my mother prepared it to celebrate my high school graduation. Mom labored for quite a while and paid dearly for the precious strands of saffron she bought to tint and flavor the dish. Thanks to a rotisserie chicken and packaged saffron rice, I can quickly get a very good paella on the table in no time and for a lot less money.

3 tablespoons olive oil

1 large onion, chopped (about 1 cup)

½ large red bell pepper, chopped (about ½ cup)

½ large green bell pepper, chopped (about ½ cup)

½ pound Spanish chorizo or kielbasa, sliced into ¼-inch pieces

1 tablespoon jarred minced garlic

2 (5-ounce) packages saffron rice (about 1½ cups of rice)

2 teaspoons dried oregano, crumbled between the fingers

1 (14½-ounce) can fat-free less-sodium chicken broth (about 1¾ cups)

1½ cups water

1½ cups bite-size chunks rotisserie chicken

1 cup frozen peeled cooked shrimp (about 100 per pound)

1 cup frozen peas

3 tablespoons finely chopped flat-leaf (Italian) parsley

Pepper, to taste

1. Heat the oil in a 12-inch nonstick skillet over medium-high heat. Add the onion and bell peppers, and cook, stirring frequently, until they begin to soften, about 5 minutes. Add the chorizo and garlic, and cook, stirring frequently, until the sausage just begins to brown, about 3 minutes. Add the rice and oregano, and cook for 1 minute, stirring frequently. Add the broth and water. Stir well and bring to a boil. Turn the heat to low, cover, and simmer for 15 minutes, stirring frequently.

2. Add the chicken, shrimp, and peas. Stir well and simmer, covered, until the rice is tender but

not mushy, the shrimp is warm, and the flavors have melded, about 10 minutes. Stir occasionally. Stir in the parsley and pepper.

Company's Coming: Make two batches for a meal that will thrill your guests.

RUSTIC PASTA PRIMAVERA

—Makes 4 servings—

———— 🥄🍴 ————

This simple, everyday pasta is an easy dinner to get on the table on busy nights since you can put the sauce together while the penne cooks. The broccoli has a pleasant roasted flavor from cooking in the skillet. With chicken and fresh vegetables already in the pasta, just add a baguette to complete this satisfying meal.

8 ounces uncooked penne (about 3 cups)

SPICE BLEND

1½ teaspoons dried basil, crumbled between
   the fingers
1½ teaspoons dried oregano, crumbled
   between the fingers

½ teaspoon salt
¼ teaspoon red pepper flakes

SAUCE

3 tablespoons olive oil
3 cups bite-size broccoli florets (about 1
   large bunch)
1 large red pepper, cut into ¼-inch strips
   and cut in half crosswise
1 (6-ounce) package sliced mushrooms (about
   2 cups)

2 teaspoons jarred minced garlic
2 cups bite-size chunks rotisserie chicken,
   pulled apart by hand
½ cup fat-free less-sodium chicken broth
½ cup dry white wine or dry vermouth
Pepper, to taste
½ cup already-shredded Parmesan cheese

1. Cook the pasta according to package directions, just until tender. Keep warm.

2. **MAKE THE SPICE BLEND:** Meanwhile, stir the ingredients together in a small bowl and set aside.

3. **MAKE THE SAUCE:** Heat the oil in a 12-inch nonstick skillet over medium-high heat. Add the broccoli florets and cook for 2 minutes, stirring frequently. Add the bell pepper and cook until the broccoli is crisp-tender and the bell pepper has softened slightly, about 2 minutes. Stir to prevent sticking. The broccoli should begin to brown.

4. Lower the heat to medium. Add the mushrooms, garlic, and spice blend. Cook, stirring constantly, until the mushrooms start to lose their juice and turn a very light brown, about 2 minutes. Add the chicken, broth, wine, and pepper. Bring to a simmer, stirring frequently. Pour the sauce over the drained pasta and toss well. Serve with the cheese.

In a Pinch: No wine on hand? Use 1 cup chicken broth and a squeeze of fresh lemon juice instead.

Serve It Up: Serve the pasta in a warm bowl for a special touch. Run hot water into the bowl, pour out, then pat the bowl dry.

BASMATI AND DRIED FRUIT PILAF

—Makes 4 servings—

Dried fruit and chicken pair with basmati rice to bring a hint of the exotic to this main dish pilaf. You can substitute long grain white rice for the basmati. The dish will be very good, but not as fragrant. This is an easy, family pleasing meal.

SPICE BLEND

½ teaspoon ground cinnamon
¼ teaspoon ground nutmeg
¼ teaspoon salt, or to taste

PILAF

2 tablespoons butter
½ small onion, finely chopped
1 cup basmati rice
1 (14½-ounce) can fat-free less-sodium chicken broth (about 1¾ cups)
¼ cup water
2 cups bite-size chunks rotisserie chicken

3 tablespoons orange juice concentrate, thawed
⅓ cup dried cranberries
⅓ cup raisins
8 dried apricot halves, cut into small pieces (about ⅓ cup)

1. **MAKE THE SPICE BLEND:** Stir the ingredients together in a small bowl and set aside.

2. **MAKE THE PILAF:** Melt the butter in a 3-quart saucepan over medium heat. Add the onion and cook until it begins to soften, about 3 minutes, stirring frequently. Reduce the heat to low and add the rice and the spice blend. Stir and cook for 3 minutes, stirring constantly. The spices will be fragrant. Add the broth, water, and chicken. Increase the heat to medium and bring to a boil. Stir well, cover, and reduce the heat to low. Simmer, covered, for 15 minutes, or

until the rice is tender. Almost all of the moisture will have evaporated. Remove from the heat, immediately stir in the remaining ingredients, and cover. Let rest for 5 minutes. Serve immediately.

▶ Notes

- I used an American basmati that did not require rinsing before cooking. Check the label of your rice; you may need to rinse it before you cook it.
- Not sure when almost all of the moisture has evaporated when you are cooking rice? Look at the side of the pot. If very little steam is coming out of the side, most of the moisture has evaporated.

IN A PINCH: Substitute 1 cup of a dried chopped fruit mix for the cranberries, raisins, and apricots.

ROASTED ASPARAGUS LEMON FETTUCCINE ALFREDO

—Makes 4 servings—

You can dine in elegance in no time with a rotisserie chicken and a combination of roasting the asparagus and walnuts, and spiking a ready-to-use Alfredo sauce with a touch of freshly-squeezed lemon juice. Make this in the spring when asparagus is plentiful.

1 (16-ounce) jar Alfredo sauce

12 ounces dried fettuccine

1 pound medium-width fresh asparagus, trimmed of tough ends and cut into 2-inch pieces (about 3 cups)

2 medium shallots, peeled and thinly sliced (about ¼ cup)

3 tablespoons olive oil

2 cups bite-size chunks rotisserie chicken, skin removed

⅔ cup coarsely chopped walnut pieces

Salt, to taste

⅓ cup freshly-squeezed lemon juice

Pepper, to taste

½ cup already-shredded Parmesan cheese (optional)

1. Place a rack in the center of the oven and preheat the oven to 450° F. Pour the Alfredo sauce into a 4-cup microwaveable container. Set aside.

2. Prepare the fettuccine according to package directions. Drain, return to the pot, and cover to keep warm.

3. While the fettuccine cooks, lightly coat a 13 × 9-inch glass pan with nonstick cooking spray. Toss the asparagus, shallots, and oil together in the pan. Spread in a single layer and roast until the asparagus softens, about 10 minutes. Add the chicken and walnuts, sprinkle lightly with salt, and stir well. Roast 5 more minutes to lightly toast the walnuts, stirring occasionally.

4. Spoon the asparagus mixture over the pasta and toss well to combine. Microwave the Alfredo sauce on high power until it just begins to boil, about 2 minutes. Stir in the lemon juice. Pour over the pasta, toss well, and season with salt and pepper. Serve immediately, sprinkling with cheese if desired.

Company's Coming: This is a great way to have another couple over with a maximum of appeal and a minimum of work.

Lighter Touch: Use a light Alfredo sauce.

PINEAPPLE FRIED RICE

—Makes 4–6 servings—

Speckled with sweet, juicy pineapple chunks and tender raisins, this delectable version of one of my favorite Thai fried rices brings a touch of the exotic to your table in no time. I really prefer the flavor and fragrance of jasmine rice in this dish, but plain white rice will do in a pinch. Cook the rice while you are having dinner the night before since it fries much better cold.

3 tablespoons vegetable oil, divided
2 eggs, beaten with a pinch of salt
1 bunch green onions, sliced (about 1 cup)
½ cup cashews (optional)
2 teaspoons jarred minced garlic
1 cup frozen cooked shrimp (about 100 per pound), thawed
1 tablespoon Asian fish sauce (nam pla)
1 tablespoon soy sauce

4 cups cooked jasmine rice, chilled (about 1 cup raw)
1½ cups large shreds rotisserie chicken, skin removed and meat pulled apart by hand
⅓ cup small bite-size cubes deli ham
⅓ cup raisins
1 (8-ounce) can pineapple chunks in juice, drained (about ½ cup)

1. Lightly coat a 12-inch nonstick skillet with cooking spray. Add 1 tablespoon oil and place over medium heat. Add the eggs and cook until they are just set, pushing and turning with a spatula. Remove the pan from the heat, scoop the eggs onto a plate, and break them into pieces. Wipe the skillet clean.

2. Return the skillet to the stove over medium-high heat. Add the remaining 2 tablespoons oil, heat for 1 minute, and then add the onions, cashews if using, and garlic. Cook for 2 minutes, stirring constantly. Add the shrimp and cook 2 more minutes, turning constantly to color the shrimp evenly and prevent the cashews and garlic from burning. Add the fish sauce and soy sauce and stir well. Spoon in the rice and stir well to combine. Add the chicken, ham, and

raisins, and cook for 3–4 minutes to heat through, stirring constantly. Stir in the pineapple and eggs, and cook for 2 more minutes, stirring constantly. Serve immediately.

▶ Notes

- Nam pla is a salty fish sauce with a distinctive odor. The splash used in this recipe adds a subtle flavor to the dish. Nam pla is used in Thai cooking much as soy sauce is used in Chinese cooking. Look for it in the Asian food aisle of the grocery store or in a Thai market.
- Take the shrimp out of the freezer the night before and refrigerate it in a plastic bag. Or put the shrimp in a colander in the sink and run hot water over them to quick-thaw.

Just You or Two: This reheats well, so don't worry about leftovers.

Company's Coming: Spoon the rice into a hollowed-out pineapple for a dramatic, authentic presentation. Cut across 2 inches down from the crown of the pineapple to make a lid. Cut around the interior of the pineapple about 1 inch from the outside. Insert a sharp knife in spots about 2 inches from the base and cut back and forth to loosen the bottom. Pull the pineapple flesh out, and remove and discard the core. Chop the rest of the pineapple into chunks and use about $1/2$ cup instead of the canned pineapple. Keep the rest for another time. To serve, spoon the rice into the pineapple shell, put the top on, and wait for the ooh's and aah's.

SAY "MORE, PLEASE" LASAGNA IN A POT

—Makes about 6–8 servings—

This stir-in-one dinner is great when you want the flavors and creaminess of lasagna but do not want to turn on the oven. My recipe tester, Maria, suggested using bow-tie pasta. They work just great and are easy to eat. This is a kid favorite, and you are likely to hear requests for more.

PASTA

12 ounces bow-tie pasta
1 (15-ounce) container part-skim ricotta cheese (about 2 cups)
½ teaspoon ground nutmeg

SAUCE

1 tablespoon olive oil
½ pound Italian sausage, removed from casing
1 large onion, chopped (about 1 cup)
1 tablespoon jarred minced garlic
1 (28-ounce) jar pasta sauce
1 (8-ounce) can Italian-style tomato sauce

1 (10-ounce) package frozen chopped spinach, broken into smaller pieces
2½–3 cups bite-size chunks rotisserie chicken
½ teaspoon salt, or to taste
1 cup already-shredded mozzarella cheese
½ cup already-shredded Parmesan cheese

1. **MAKE THE PASTA:** Cook the pasta in a large pot according to package directions until it is almost tender to the bite. Drain, return to the pot, and immediately stir in the ricotta and nutmeg. Set aside.

2. **MAKE THE SAUCE:** While the pasta is cooking, heat the oil in a 12-inch nonstick skillet over medium heat. Add the sausage, onion, and garlic. Break the sausage into pieces and cook,

stirring frequently, until there is no pink left, about 8 minutes. Add the pasta sauce and tomato sauce, stir, and bring to a simmer, stirring frequently. Add the spinach and cook until the spinach breaks apart, about 5 minutes. Stir frequently to help break it into pieces. Stir in the chicken and salt, turn the heat to low, and simmer, uncovered, for 10 minutes to blend the flavors.

3. Carefully pour the sauce over the pasta and stir well. Cook over low heat just long enough to bring to a simmer. Stir in the cheeses and warm just long enough to melt them. Serve immediately.

GREAT GLAZES

What a difference a glaze makes! A simple dinner of rotisserie chicken quickly becomes delicious dining with the flavor boosts these glazes and sauces offer. A glaze does not have to be time-consuming. A tasty glaze can be as simple as stirring thawed frozen orange juice concentrate (about 3 tablespoons) into honey (about ⅓ cup) and brushing it over the chicken and baking until the sauce is bubbly. The recipes in this chapter add the quick zip you need to transform a rotisserie chicken into a special occasion. There are a lot of great bottled sauces available in the markets. If time is truly tight, open a bottle of your favorite sauce or glaze to dress up the chicken.

You have a number of handy choices for quickly glazing or saucing a rotisserie chicken:

- Put a whole chicken or chicken pieces in a pan coated with nonstick cooking spray. Brush the sauce or glaze over the chicken and heat in a 350 degree oven until the chicken is hot and the sauce is nice and bubbly, basting occasionally.
- Put chicken pieces in a pan coated with nonstick cooking spray. Spoon sauce over the chicken and microwave until the chicken is hot.
- Preheat the broiler, line a pan with foil and lightly coat the foil with nonstick cooking spray. Put the chicken pieces on the pan skin side down, brush with glaze, and heat 3–4 minutes. Turn, brush the other side with glaze, and heat another 3–4 minutes, being careful not to burn the glaze.

With these recipes you can make a basic rotisserie chicken a meal no matter how tight your time is. Just douse an already-roasted chicken with homemade Apricot Ginger Glaze or serve a little Mustard Caper Sauce alongside, set the table, and suddenly your everyday rotisserie chicken dinner will not seem so everyday anymore.

HOMEMADE GRAVY

—Makes about 2 cups—

Rich homemade gravy can quickly elevate a rotisserie chicken to special status. It takes only a few minutes to stir this together, but it will seem as if you cooked for hours. I learned to make a gravy watching my father patiently stir the flour and oil into a nice roux, then just as patiently stir in the liquid. Patience pays off with a delicious, smooth gravy.

SPICE BLEND

½ teaspoon dried thyme, crumbled between the fingers

½ teaspoon onion powder

¼ teaspoon garlic powder

¼ teaspoon salt

⅛ teaspoon pepper

BASE

¼ cup vegetable oil

3 tablespoons all-purpose flour

1 (14½-ounce) can fat-free less-sodium chicken broth (about 1¾ cups), contents warmed

Drippings from chicken container and inside chicken

3 tablespoons half-and-half

1. **MAKE THE SPICE BLEND:** Stir the ingredients together in a small bowl and set aside.

2. **MAKE THE BASE:** Heat the oil in a small saucepan over medium heat. Add the flour and cook, stirring constantly, until it turns a very light brown, about 3 minutes. Add the spice blend, stir, and cook for 1 minute, stirring constantly. Slowly stir in the broth, stirring constantly. Make sure the mixture is smooth before you add any more liquid. Stir in the drippings and bring to a boil. Turn the heat to low and simmer, uncovered, for 10 minutes, stirring frequently. Stir in the half-and-half. Heat through but do not boil. Serve immediately.

▶ Notes

- If making gravy makes you nervous, warming the broth before adding it to the flour helps make sure that lumps will not form.
- This gravy is on the thinnish side. If you like a thicker gravy, increase the flour by 1 tablespoon to ¼ cup.

ALMOST HOMEMADE GRAVY

A quick fix to a jarred gravy can be just the ticket when time is truly tight and you would like a little gravy with your rotisserie chicken. Stir in 1 tablespoon of dry white wine after the gravy simmers if you are so inclined.

1 tablespoon butter

1 small shallot, finely chopped (scant 1 tablespoon)

1 (12-ounce) jar chicken gravy

Drippings from chicken container and inside chicken

2 tablespoons milk

½ teaspoon dried thyme, crumbled

1. Melt the butter in a small saucepan over medium heat. Add the shallot and cook, stirring constantly, until it softens, about 2 minutes. Add the remaining ingredients, stir well, and bring to a simmer. Simmer until hot, about 5 minutes, stirring frequently. Serve immediately.

> **In the Microwave:** Stir the ingredients together in a microwaveable dish. Cover the dish and microwave on high for 3 minutes. Serve immediately.

> **Company's Coming:** If guests knock, simply open more jars of gravy and pull out the gravy boat with complete confidence!

APRICOT GINGER GLAZE

—Makes about 1½ cups—

—————

You can turn an ordinary rotisserie chicken into a delightful meal in under five minutes of hands-on time with this family-pleasing glaze. The sweet tang from the apricots and orange juice and the bite of ginger come together in the oven while the chicken warms. It could not be easier. Stir a handful of raisins into quick-cooking couscous for a weekday dinner in no time.

1 rotisserie chicken, cut into quarters
1 cup apricot preserves
¼ cup orange juice

1 tablespoon butter
1½ teaspoons ground ginger, or to taste
Pinch of salt

1. Preheat the oven to 350° F. Coat a 13 × 9-inch pan with nonstick spray.

2. Place the chicken in the pan. Combine the preserves, juice, butter, ginger, and salt in a small saucepan. Stir over medium heat until the preserves and butter are melted, about 1 minute. Spoon on enough glaze to cover the chicken. Reserve any leftover glaze for serving time. Bake until the glaze is thick and bubbly and the chicken is hot, about 20 minutes, basting 2 or 3 times. Heat any extra glaze and pass it at the table.

VARIATION

Moroccan Spice Glaze:

Reduce the ginger to ½ teaspoon and add ½ teaspoon ground cinnamon, ½ teaspoon of ground cumin, and a pinch of cayenne.

YUMMY CRANBERRY CHICKEN

—Makes 4 servings—

———— 🥄🍴 ————

Why serve the cranberry sauce and the chicken separately when you can enjoy the two of them in one? Melting down cranberry sauce makes it Thanksgiving any time of year. Our three-year-old screeched "yummy" the first time he tasted this, and I am betting that your children will, too.

1 (16-ounce) can whole berry cranberry sauce

2 tablespoons frozen orange juice concentrate, thawed

2 tablespoons butter

½ teaspoon ground ginger

½ teaspoon dried thyme, crumbled between the fingers

¼ teaspoon ground cinnamon

1 (4-ounce) container mixed fruit cup, drained (about ½ cup)

⅓ cup chopped walnuts (optional)

1 rotisserie chicken, cut into serving pieces

1. Lightly coat a microwaveable pan that is large enough to hold the chicken pieces with non-stick cooking spray.

2. Place the cranberry sauce in the pan, break it into pieces, and add the orange juice concentrate, butter, ginger, thyme, and cinnamon. Mix well. Cover and microwave on full power until the sauce begins to soften, about 5 minutes.

3. Add the mixed fruit and walnuts, if using. Stir well to combine. Place the chicken in the pan and spoon the sauce over the top. Cover and microwave on medium power until the chicken is warm, about 3 minutes.

▶ Note

- Stir in 1 tablespoon Grand Marnier along with the fruit if you have it on hand.

Lighter Touch: Reduce the butter to 1 tablespoon. Remove the skin from the chicken before putting it in the pan.

SLOW-COOKING BARBECUE CHICKEN

—Makes 4 servings—

This is a variation on my family's vinegar-based recipe for barbecue sauce. The appetizing blend of citrus and barbecue flavors has graced many a barbecue chicken in our house over the years. Don't be concerned about the long list of ingredients. It takes just a few minutes to stir together, and melt-in-your-mouth goodness is yours a few hours later.

1 rotisserie chicken, cut into quarters

1 large onion, peeled and sliced into ¼-inch rounds (about 1 cup)

2 (¼-inch-thick) lemon slices, peel on and seeds removed

1 cup ketchup

3 tablespoons packed brown sugar

2 tablespoons cider vinegar

2 tablespoons honey

2 tablespoons Worcestershire sauce

1 tablespoon Dijon mustard

1 tablespoon butter, cut into pieces

2 teaspoons jarred minced garlic

½ teaspoon pepper

¼ cup water

1. Place the chicken in the slow cooker, skin side up, preferably in a single layer. Top with the onion and lemon slices. Stir the remaining ingredients together in a small bowl and pour over the chicken. Cook on low or medium-low for 4–5 hours, according to the manufacturer's directions.

VARIATION

For barbecue chicken in the oven, preheat the oven to 400° F and place the chicken in a baking pan coated with nonstick cooking spray. Pour about 2 cups of your favorite bottled barbecue sauce over the chicken and bake, covered, until the chicken is hot and the sauce is bubbly, about 20 minutes.

In a Pinch: Place the chicken in the slow cooker, top with the onion slices, and pour about 2 cups of your favorite bottled barbecue sauce over the chicken. Cook on low heat for about 4 hours.

Company's Coming: Stock up on rotisserie chickens and bottled barbecue sauce, pull out the roasting pan, and invite friends for an easy backyard picnic.

MUSTARD CAPER SAUCE

—Makes about 1½ cups—

———— ✶ ————

Here is a simple and enticing way to dress up a warm or cold rotisserie chicken.

1 (8-ounce) container light sour cream (about
   1 cup)
⅓ cup milk

5 tablespoons Dijon mustard
2 tablespoons capers, drained
¼ teaspoon white pepper

1. Combine the sour cream and milk in a small saucepan. Warm over medium heat until the sour cream melts and the mixture is hot, about 2 minutes, stirring frequently. Stir in the mustard, capers, and pepper. Spoon over hot or cold chicken pieces.

MAPLE ROSEMARY GLAZE

—Makes about ¾ cup—

— 🥄🍴 —

Use pure maple syrup not pancake syrup for this perfect fall glaze. Pancake syrups have other sweeteners and you want pure maple flavor. Serve with wild rice.

1 rotisserie chicken, whole
½ cup pure maple syrup
2 tablespoons pure apple juice
1 tablespoon butter

1 small shallot, finely chopped (about 1 tablespoon)
¼ teaspoon dried rosemary, crumbled between the fingers

1. Preheat the oven to 350° F. Lightly coat a 13 × 9-inch pan with nonstick cooking spray. Place the chicken in the pan. Stir the maple syrup, apple juice, butter, shallot, and rosemary together in a small saucepan and place over high heat. Bring to a boil, then lower the heat to maintain a gentle boil. Boil for 8–10 minutes, stirring frequently. The mixture will thicken.

2. Brush the hot mixture over the chicken. Bake until the chicken is hot and the glaze is bubbly, about 20 minutes, basting 2 or 3 times.

VARIATION

Maple Apple Chicken:

Cut 2 large tart apples into 8 chunks each. Place the chunks around the chicken. Brush the hot glaze over the chicken and drizzle it over the apples. Bake as directed above.

Just You or Two: Make half as much glaze. Carve the two sides of the breast from the chicken. Remove the skin, put in a small baking dish, and brush with the glaze. You will have some glaze left. Bake in a 350° F oven until the chicken is hot and the glaze is bubbly, about 15 minutes.

Company's Coming: Light the candles and invite a special guest over for the Maple Chicken Breasts with wild rice and whole green beans.

CHICKEN IN SWEET BASIL SAUCE

—Makes 4 servings—

This easier-than-easy dish takes advantage of the convenience of Alfredo sauce in a jar and always at-the-ready dried herbs to put a luscious meal on the table in a hurry. Look for a sauce with real cream. If the chicken you have on hand has a flavor that will not work well with the sauce, just remove the skin before pouring on the sauce.

1 cold rotisserie chicken, cut into serving pieces
1 tablespoon dried sweet basil, crumbled between the fingers
1 (16-ounce) jar Alfredo sauce

1. Preheat the oven to 375° F. Lightly coat a baking dish with nonstick cooking spray. Place the chicken in the pan. Stir the basil into the Alfredo sauce. Pour over the chicken and bake, covered, until the sauce is bubbly and the chicken is heated through, about 35 minutes. Or heat in the microwave until hot and bubbly.

▶ Note
- You can serve this alongside angel hair pasta tossed with a little olive oil and sliced vine-ripened tomatoes.

Lighter Touch: Look for a light Alfredo sauce.

Just You or Two: Stir 1 1/2 teaspoons basil into half a jar of sauce. Pour over the chicken and bake.

Play It Again: Shred any leftover chicken, stir it into the sauce, and toss with hot fettucine and sautéed mushrooms for a scrumptious fettucine Alfredo.

Company's Coming: You can have this on the table minutes after unexpected guests ring the doorbell.

SIZZLING SIDE DISHES

A whole rotisserie chicken can easily take center stage for a quick and easy meal on a platter. Although a whole nicely roasted chicken is indisputably a thing of beauty, you may not have the time to roast one at home. No need to panic. The market has done it for you. In this chapter I offer side dishes and some garnishing tips that will help make the meal complete.

Think variety in color, shape, and texture when you think of side dishes to accompany a rotisserie chicken. And think simple. You can easily toss quartered button mushrooms in olive oil and add a sprinkling of salt and crushed thyme leaves. Spoon them around the chicken and pop in a 350° F oven to warm the chicken and roast the mushrooms. Or you can arrange quartered oranges around the chicken on the platter and spoon your favorite rice alongside for a different touch. Fresh herbs are one of my favorite effortless ways to make a rotisserie chicken special. I simply surround the warmed chicken with sprigs of parsley, rosemary, or thyme, or a mix of herbs.

So pull out your platter and have some fun with these side dishes. Spoon the roasted potatoes alongside the chicken, tuck the apricot rice or sausage and mushroom stuffing inside the warm chicken, or simply pick a side dish and serve it from a bowl. Remember that a special side dish can quickly make the chicken more special, too.

APRICOT RICE

—Makes 4 servings—

This quick side dish is a family-pleasing dish in a hurry. The apricots and spices give it what I like to call an "exotic flair" with very little effort.

SPICE BLEND

½ teaspoon ground cinnamon
½ teaspoon ground ginger

½ teaspoon salt
¼ teaspoon ground allspice

RICE

2 (3½-ounce) packets boil-in-bag brown rice (about 5 cups cooked)
½ bunch green onions, thinly sliced (about ½ cup)

½ cup golden raisins
⅓ cup apricot preserves
⅓ cup slivered almonds (optional)
2 tablespoons butter

1. **MAKE THE SPICE BLEND:** Stir the ingredients together in a small bowl and set aside.

2. **MAKE THE RICE:** Prepare the rice according to package directions. Spoon the hot rice into a bowl and immediately stir in the spice blend, onions, raisins, preserves, almonds, if using, and butter. Fluff with a fork and serve.

RANCH MASHED POTATOES

—Makes 4 servings—

Homemade mashed potatoes are always welcome at the table with rotisserie chicken. The packaged dip seasoning and the microwave get these ready in a hurry. Mash with a handheld potato masher, a mixer, or even a serving fork. Do not put them in the food processor, however, or they will turn to paste.

3 medium russet potatoes (about 2 pounds), peeled and cut into 1-inch cubes (about 6 cups)
¼ cup milk

2 tablespoons butter
1 (4-ounce) package dry ranch dip mix
Pepper, to taste

1. Place the potatoes in a pan with just enough water to cover. Place over high heat and bring to a boil. Lower the heat, partially cover, and simmer until tender when pierced with a fork, 10–15 minutes.

2. When the potatoes are done, heat the milk and butter in the microwave, covered, on full power until the milk is hot and the butter is melted, about 2 minutes. Stir in the ranch dip mix. Set aside.

3. Drain the potatoes and return to the pot. Add the hot milk mixture and mash until you have the desired consistency. Add pepper. Stir to thoroughly combine the ingredients. Serve immediately.

SUNDAY SAUSAGE AND MUSHROOM STUFFING

—Makes 4 servings—

— 🍴 —

This stuffing is a real winner—good enough for Sunday and easy enough for any day. As a child I sat in the kitchen with my sisters and southern-transplant mother crumbling freshly baked corn bread when we made dressing. These days I add my mother's touches to a good boxed corn bread stuffing mix and sit down to a delicious dinner much faster. The smell of onion, celery, and sausage wafting though the house will say "special stuffing" to everyone.

3 tablespoons butter or vegetable oil
½ small onion, finely chopped
1 rib celery, finely chopped
6 ounces bulk breakfast sausage
1 cup sliced mushrooms
2 teaspoons jarred minced garlic

½ teaspoon poultry seasoning
1 (6-ounce) box corn bread stuffing mix
1 (14½-ounce) can fat-free less-sodium chicken broth (about 1¾ cups)
¼ cup water

1. Melt the butter in a 12-inch nonstick skillet over medium-high heat. Add the onion and celery, and cook, stirring frequently, just until they begin to soften, about 3 minutes. Add the sausage and mushrooms. Cook until the sausage is no longer pink, stirring frequently to break up the sausage, and cook the mushrooms and sausage evenly, about 5 minutes. Drain off any excess fat. Add the garlic and poultry seasoning, and cook for 2 minutes, stirring constantly.

2. Add the stuffing mix, broth, and water. Stir well and bring to a boil. Turn the heat to low and simmer just until the liquid is absorbed, about 3 minutes.

VARIATION

Baked Dressing:

If you would like a crisper stuffing, try this variation. Preheat the oven to 350° F. Wrap the skillet handle with foil if it is not ovenproof. Spread the stuffing evenly in the pan and bake until it is slightly firm to the touch, about 15 minutes.

▶ **Note**

- If you are so inclined, you can spoon the stuffing into the warmed chicken and put the chicken on a platter for a special presentation.

CORN SUCCOTASH

—Makes 4 servings—

Lightly fried corn makes a quick and tasty alternative to boiled corn as a side dish for rotisserie chicken in this takeoff on a Cajun favorite, maque choux. The vegetable medley makes this a refreshing and colorful addition to the table.

SPICE BLEND

2 teaspoons paprika
1 teaspoon dried thyme, crumbled between the fingers

1 teaspoon salt
½ teaspoon pepper

CORN

2 tablespoons vegetable oil
1 large onion, chopped (about 1 cup)
1 green bell pepper, chopped (about 1 cup)
1 tablespoon jarred minced garlic

2½ cups frozen corn kernels
1 (14½-ounce) can diced tomatoes in juice, drained

1. **MAKE THE SPICE BLEND:** Stir the ingredients together in a small bowl and set aside.

2. **PREPARE THE CORN:** Heat the oil in a 12-inch nonstick skillet over medium-high heat. Add the onion and bell pepper, and cook, stirring occasionally, until the vegetables begin to soften, about 4 minutes. Add the garlic and spice blend, and cook for 2 minutes, stirring constantly. Add the corn and tomatoes, stir well, and cook until hot and the flavors are blended, about 5 minutes.

VARIATION

For a great main course, stir in 2 cups of bite-size chunks of rotisserie chicken along with the corn and tomatoes. Add liquid pepper sauce to taste.

GARLIC ROASTED POTATOES

I learned to make these at my first restaurant job in Berkeley, California, more than twenty years ago and have been serving them to family and friends ever since. Simple and great, they are a welcome addition to a rotisserie chicken meal. I do not give proportions here; make as many as you need and season to your family's taste. The cooking time depends on the size of the potatoes, so check them after 25 minutes or so.

Small red potatoes, scrubbed and patted dry
Head of garlic, cloves separated but unpeeled
Dried rosemary, crumbled between the fingers
Olive oil

Salt, preferably kosher

1. Preheat the oven to 450° F. Choose a roasting pan large enough to hold the potatoes in a single layer. Line with foil, shiny side down. Place the potatoes in the pan, scatter with the garlic cloves, and sprinkle a few rosemary leaves on top. Drizzle with just enough oil to coat. Turn the potatoes to coat with the oil. Lightly sprinkle salt over all. Bake until the potatoes are tender when pierced with a fork, 30–40 minutes. Squeeze the garlic onto the potatoes when eating.

▶ Note
   • If the potatoes are large, cut them into quarters before baking.

Lighter Touch: Substitute olive oil spray for the olive oil.

INDEX